# Dr. Paul A. Jones

# THE MYTH OF REHABILITATION

### (SECOND PRINTING)

outskirtspress

DENVER, COLORADO

The Myth of Rehabilitation
(Second Printing)
All Rights Reserved.
Copyright © 2013 Dr. Paul A. Jones
v4.0

Originally published by Scripta Humanistica, 1383 Kersey Lane, Potomac, Maryland 20854 U.S.A. (ISBN No. 1-882528-34-4, Volume 144). Scripta Humanistic is directed by Bruno M. Damiani of the Catholic University of America.

Outskirts Press, Inc.
http://www.outskirtspress.com

ISBN: 978-1-4787-1304-3

Registration: TX 7-528-107

# *Acknowledgments*

The author would like to thank his family, friends, and various colleagues for their encouragement in writing this book. Deserving of special consideration are my wife, Frances, who helped with the typing and offered several suggestions; my sister, Cynthia, who edited the manuscript and also offered many helpful suggestions; my father, Paul, who was very supportive during the entire process; and my brother, Philip who also offered encouragement. The author also expresses thanks to Doctors Brad Hyde and Bruno Damiani for their helpful suggestions.

Many others, too numerous to mention, have been helpful over the years in providing the concepts and information that have prompted this author to express the ideas found in this book. These include professionals and para-professionals from many disciplines, as well as many inmates and ex-inmates.

# TABLE OF CONTENTS

# INTRODUCTION

BASICALLY, REHABILITATION IS a myth. However, the belief in its effectiveness has been around for quite a while. Socially conscious people such as Jane Adams are primarily responsible for its widespread acceptance. Of course, rehabilitation is a nice sounding concept. Who does not want to help those who have gone astray because of lack of opportunities or other reasons? We want them to get a new lease on life and become good, productive citizens. The problem is that this change usually does not happen.

As I state in Chapter I, and several other places in the book, most criminals are sociopaths. And a major characteristic of sociopaths is an inability to change. They have an unwillingness to follow social norms of behavior, and they lack any feelings or concern for others. These and other attitudes are formed very early in life to cope with a harsh or neglectful environment (McConnell, 1989). Lack of proper parental care and nurturing can usually be shown to be the cause. However, while sociopathic attitudes can be increased and reinforced in a continuing undesirable environment, little can be done to reverse them even in a good environment at a later time. Also, while it is probably true that "bad" prisons can make people worse for a variety of reasons, so called "good" prisons with active rehabilitation programs do not make them better. Mistreat a sociopath, or anyone else while he or she is in prison, and they will most likely become more hostile and more anti-social—and consequently more danger-ous if and when they are released. Nevertheless, rehabilitation, more properly called reform, just does not work. Although occasionally there are cases of people who seem to have turned their lives around, this does not happen very often, contrary to what many would like to believe. And when it does happen, the person himself does the changing, but not because of some externally applied counseling or therapy.

Other contributors to the rehabilitation myth are the prison do-gooders, many of whom are just prison groupies. They are a nuisance and serve no useful purpose, at least not as far as prisons are con-cerned. They need to be prevented from visiting prisons or even writing inmates.

Chapter IV discusses Brain Mapping, Genetics, and DNA banks. Brain mapping is relatively new, but already it can be used for medi-cal diagnoses (ICBM, 1997). Eventually, it may be useful in diagnosing psychoses, a variety of other mental problems, and sociopathology as well. And then true reform may actually be possible—by altering the brain surgically, chemically, or electronically. Another benefit could be that, along with Sodium Pentothal interviews, we could solve many unsolved crimes. Of course, we may have to rethink our out-dated beliefs regarding self-incrimination. A person knows if he has killed someone, and he also knows where the body is located. By tapping the correct part of the brain, he could be induced to reveal both facts.

There are cases today where the authorities are certain that some-one has committed a crime, such as murder or kidnapping, but there is not enough usable evidence for a conviction. The man in Atlanta who shot up two offices, killing several people, is one example. The police are fairly certain that he is the one who killed his former wife and his mother-in-law (CBS).[1] He, of course, denied it and came up with an alibi. Since the authorities could not use a Pentothal interview and a lie detector test, (plus not having brain mapping available), the system allowed him to get away with murder. Our Bill Of Rights is a wonderful thing. However, it is over two hundred years old, and it needs to be updated. We must continue to protect the rights of the accused, but we also need to stop the gimmicks that guilty people use to beat the system.

While sociopaths are produced by undesirable environments, other problem people seem to be the result of genetics, at least to some extent. Autism, schizophrenia, manic depression and various other disorders are in this category. Some , although not all, of these people can also be criminal or violent. Hopefully, in the future, the specific genes involved can be identified and used for diagnosis, classification and treatment—as with brain mapping. DNA banks would enable the authorities to link people with specific crimes already committed. But more important, we could know in advance who might be inclined to commit certain types of crimes. While using DNA banks and brain mapping in this manner may seem somewhat far-fetched and futuristic, it is much more realistic than trying to rehabilitate the unreformable.

# REHABILITATION

## A. The Belief in Rehabilitation

WHILE IN COLLEGE and graduate school, I read several articles and write-ups about the negative aspects of the American criminal justice system, but it all seemed academic, not something that applied to every day life. However, when I went to work for the Tennessee Department of Corrections in 1975 as a work release counselor, and later as a teacher, a guard and as a Chaplain, I soon became aware of several faults or weaknesses in the system. Our courts allow escape risks out on bond (like Ira Einhorn from Pittsburgh, who still has not been brought to justice 30 years after killing his girlfriend and putting her body in a trunk) (CBS, 2000, June 1).[1] Parole boards release murderers and violent sex offenders, such as Kenneth Allen McDuff (Lavergene, 1999) and Arthur Shawcross, to again prey on the public. Shawcross, who murdered two children, was released after only 15 Years (Wilson, 1995, p. 331) (which is absurd), and in no time at all he began killing women, for a total of at least ten. I also found the ridiculously light sentences often given for terrible crimes to be surprising, especially when reduced even more by parole boards.

Another weakness is the insanity defense, which in itself is insane, and probably should be eliminated. Most of those who have used it successfully to "beat the charge" altogether, or at least to be sent to a hospital instead of a prison, are not insane nor were they temporarily insane at the time of the crime. On the other hand, I met several inmates who obviously were insane; nevertheless, they ended up with long prison terms. Often those that the insanity defense was meant to help do not get to use it, while those who do use it successfully are seemingly just manipulating the system (Caplain, 1984, p. 336).

One aspect of the criminal justice system that especially bothered me was all the emphasis on rehabilitation. In spite of all the enthusiasm for it in some quarters, I soon realized that it was basically a joke. There were educational programs, counseling programs, and many other things that were totally ineffective as far as changing any inmates for the better. Of course, prisoners liked the TV's, stereos, and other things that were fun or enjoyable, but these things certainly were not making them better people. I was also concerned that so many people not connected with prisons actually believed in and supported the entire rehabilitation concept.

In August of 1998, I turned on the television set (ABC Nightline). A well known commentator and a prominent leader were discussing American prisons. Although both men were obviously intelligent and well educated, they continued to discuss the need for more and better methods of rehabilitation for prisoners, as though rehabilitation actually existed. Unfortunately, this misapprehension is not unusual. Many intelligent people believe that rehabilitating criminals is actually possible.[2]

In spite of the fact that many, and probably most, criminals are sociopaths, and sociopaths do not (in fact cannot) change or reform, this pervasive belief in the possibility and desirability of rehabilitation continues to affect many of our laws and to influence much of what we do in social work and in the criminal justice system. Social workers, judges, parole officers, psychologists, and many others who should know better still believe in the rehabilitation myth. However, just because we would like for something to be true does not make it so. We would like for all sick people to get well, but of course, they do not. In would also be nice if we could "cure" or "fix" all criminals, but it just does not happen.

This idea that we should attempt to rehabilitate convicted felons has been around for quite a while. The assumptions are that it can be done, that we should do it, and that criminals are entitled to have it done for or to them (Menninger, 1968). All three of these assumptions are false. To try to rehabilitate or reform criminals is basically useless because it is impossible. Also, if we are going to try to change or improve people, we need to do it before they get into trouble or do harmful things—not afterwards. And since we really cannot or will not change the conditions that produce the sociopath in advance, it is absurd to think we can do it after they are locked up.

While it may be true that some offenders are not sociopaths, and that in some cases they do stop repeating undesirable behaviors, it is they themselves who decide to change and not some externally applied counseling or therapy that changes them. We need to drop the entire idea of treatment or rehabilitation. If we are going to do anything at all, we need to identify the conditions that produce sociopaths and intervene in advance, not after it is too late.

## B. What Is Rehabilitation?

THE DICTIONARY DEFINES rehabilitation as restoring or returning someone to a former state of adequate or appropriate functioning. This and other similar definitions do make sense when applied to physical problems or conditions. For instance, if one injures his or her back, leg, or whatever, then exercise and/or therapy may very well help in returning the physical functioning to normal—or at least close to it. On the other hand, when talking about criminals, what is usually meant is reform—not rehabilitation. Reform means changing a bad or improperly behaving person into one who functions acceptably. However, if the person never was a properly behaving citizen, the term rehabilitation really does not apply. We are trying to change him or her, not return him to something that never existed. We need to use the word reform, not the term rehabilitation—which tends to be misleading.

Since the belief in rehabilitation is generally accepted by our society, the idea of its being a myth will probably meet with some resistance. First, we have the do-gooders who generally believe that it is desirable to help or "fix" deviant or disfunctional persons—including criminals. Then there are those who are in the rehabilitation business, such as psychiatrists, counselors, psychologists, social workers, and others who "need" to believe in rehabilitation in order to feel that their line of work is actually effective. However, as stated earlier, many, and probably most, criminals are sociopaths. This personality type is not reformable (McConnell, 1989). Therefore, to spend time, effort, and money trying to change them is basically useless, and often leads to our foolishly returning them to society where they again pose a threat to "normal" citizens.

Basically, the facts just do not justify the belief in rehabilitation. It is fairly well known that a very high percentage of criminals are repeat offenders. Probably 95% of our prison inmates are either violent or habitual offenders (Gest, 1997). Many return to prison over and over again. Those who do not return are not necessarily rehabilitated. They are probably just more skilled at not being caught, prosecuted, or convicted. The truth of the matter is that if we actually knew how to reform or change people, we would to it in advance—not after they have committed a crime or crimes.

## C. My Experience with Rehabilitation

I WENT TO work with the Tennessee Department of Corrections in 1977 as a counselor for the work release program in Knoxville, Tennessee. Later, I worked as a teacher and as a Chaplain at Brushy Mountain Prison. After moving to Huntsville, Texas in 1979, I went to work as a teacher and, for a short time, as a prison guard. I saw a lot, heard a lot, and learned a lot.

I particularly remember what one young inmate, Steve, said during a group counseling session. I often held group therapy type sessions both as a teacher and as a counselor. The inmates enjoyed them, and both they and I learned a lot. One question I posed was whether prisons were too lenient or too severe in punishing offenders. Most of the students just fumbled around with the answer, not really coming up with a clear opinion. However, one young student did voice a very definite opinion. He explained that most non-violent statutory offenders were probably treated too severely (By statutory offenders he meant those who broke the law but did not physically harm anyone.) On the other hand, he thought that most dangerous and violent criminals were dealt with far too leniently. Over the years I have come to agree on both counts.

He thought that it was absurd that murderers and other violent offenders frequently received ridculously short sentences, often only serving five, four or even less than one year in prison. At the same time, other inmates might actually do fifteen, twenty or even more years for a drug or a bad check conviction. In many cases, prisons are far too easy for bad people. Many very cruel and sadistic offenders are treated far too well, considering what they have done. Steve felt that all violent inmates should be locked in semi-solitary confinement, with no phone calls, no recreation, no mail, no visitations, no art, or anything else, as is done in Japan.[3] He believed that there should be "easy" prisons with benefits for non-violent, non-dangerous inmates. This seemed to be good thinking for a young man. Over the years I have thought of this conversation often, and although I do not remember his full name, I believe he had a much better perception of our prison system than most people do.

Working with the Tennessee prison system, I met several inmates who were sentenced to a year or less for killing someone, and I found this was quite common. Often it was outright murder, but the charge was plea-bargained down to some type of manslaughter. One man on work release had gotten into a fight in a bar. When he left and got into his truck, the other man followed him and threw a brick through his windshield. He than got out and shot the man to death. His one-year sentence was not any more absurd than the case of a man in Texas recently who had gotten into a argument with some people who were in one of his uninhabited buildings. When they tried to drive away, he shot one in the back, killing him (CBS-10). He claimed self-defense, and the jury accepted it. But, it cannot be self-defense when someone is trying to run away. Cases like this point to the need for legal reform, allowing an acquittal or an inadequate sentence to also be appealed, as it is in some other countries. Another inmate in the minimum security section of Brushy Mountain had evidently beaten his wife to death while high on drugs and alcohol. He claimed not to remember, although he did not deny doing it. He seemed like a nice guy—friendly, but quiet. He thought that he should have received a life sentence for killing his wife, if he in fact did do it. However, he also received only one year.

There are many cases of murderers who have killed again after being released from prison. An example is the case of Arthur Shawcross who was released from prison after serving only fifteen years for brutally killing two children (Wilson). It is not reasonable to turn someone like him loose—ever. He soon started a killing spree that involved at least ten women that we know about. There may have been even more. Also, consider the parole of Kenneth Allen McDuff from Texas who killed several women after his release (Lavergne). How can we release these dangerous predators to prey on society? Actually, most murderers probably should be sentenced to life imprisonment. The only exceptions should be when there is some sort of self-defense or when a victim of child abuse strikes back.

The average citizen is totally unaware of how many dangerous people there are loose among us, including those on bond, parole, or who have completed excessively short sentences. I know of many cases of inmates who were supposedly "cured" or rehabilitated according to their counselor or psychologist. Then, when paroled or released, they soon committed some new horrible crime. Well known is the case where writer Norman Mailer was instrumental in getting a convicted killer released. After his release he was successful at writing, but he also committed another murder. In another case, a man who was supposedly rehabilitated and no longer dangerous was released. Within a day this "non-violent" man went to this wife's house and beat her to death (CBS). These two examples are not unusual. Actually, they are rather typical. Incidences of released criminals who repeat violent crimes happen all the time, and still we pretend that rehabilitation works.

The problem is that when we are predisposed to believe in rehabilitation, we tend to see it when there is actually no evidence of its success. Counselors make the assessment that people are rehabilitated or "fixed" primarily based on what the clients themselves tell them. That method of assessment is basically useless (Douglas, 1995). Most sociopaths with any intelligence at all soon learn what counselors, psychologists, and others are looking for that will show evidence of rehabilitation. Excellent actors, aided by a total lack of conscience, they can easily fake remorse and show all of the positive ideas and attitudes their counselors expect (McConnell). They often talk among themselves about "faking the counselor."

Most sociopaths will always be con men, con women and liars. They will say anything and play any role to get privileges or release from confinement. And they do it very well. Unfortunately, many people are deceived, causing us to turn dangerous and violent criminals and predators loose on society. Consider again the totally absurd case of McDuff in Texas (Lavergne). He was initially sentenced to death for three murders committed in 1966. When the Supreme Court overturned death sentences in 1971, his sentence was commuted to life in prison. Then in 1988 the parole board set him free, even though he was still dangerous. Just ask the parents and loved ones of all the women he tortured and murdered how they feel about his parole. No one knows for sure how many women he raped and killed after his release in 1988. There were probably six to ten, but maybe many more. The person on the parole board who was primarily instrumental in setting McDuff free should have been fired. However, paroling volumes of inmates was the policy in Texas at that time (1989) (Cartwright, 1992). There was a similar situation in Florida, also due to overcrowding. He was eventually captured and then executed in 1999.

While employed as a Chaplain at Brushy Mountain Prison in 1977, I was contacted by a representative for the Bill Gluss Crusade (not the actual name). They wanted to present a week-long program at the prison, consisting of preaching services, testimonials, athletic events, visitations with the inmates, and a variety of other things. Several men from local churches would visit the inmates cell to cell as a follow-up.

They contacted several business leaders, political leaders, churches and civic organizations. There was a lot of support for the program. It was "politically correct" to back the idea of evangelizing or converting inmates. It was hoped that at least some of these bad people would turn into good ones. They did present some high powered evangelistic preaching services, but this did not seem to result in any positive changes in any inmates. No one came forward to be "saved." Athletes on the crusade team played basketball with the prisoners, there were a lot of interesting demonstrations by karate experts and others, and many of the inmates seemed to enjoy themselves. The counselors from the churches visited most of the inmates individually. I found out later that many inmates begged or conned money or other things from these visitors.

When we summarized the results of the entire program, we found that only one inmate in the entire prison was converted, but he actually was already a believer who had just "backslidden." He only reaffirmed or rededicated himself.

The community, the prison personnel, the local churches and others all expected a massive revival. Many of the inmates would be "saved," and then there would then be an entirely different prison population. But it seemed to me and others that the program had failed—all that time and money spent, and only one convert. However, my thinking soon changed after I looked into the program and others like it more fully. Bringing the Christian message to the inmates and trying to convert them turned out to be just a gimmick. It did not matter whether inmates were converted or not. What was important was that the staff would get money from churches and others to support the program of taking the message to prisons. Success was measured in raising enough money to keep the crusade going, to pay the salaries and expenses of those involved, not in converting inmates. The ministries of athletes, weight lifters, and others on the team, needed to be supported.

While working with the work release program in Knoxville, Tennessee as a counselor, I met a young African-American inmate. His father was a local attorney who apparently contributed to his behavior. Larry was continually getting into trouble, even while on work release. When I tried to talk with him, all I ever got was, "I believe we can beat the charge." Apparently that was his primary concern—beating the charge. There was no interest in or concern for right and wrong or good and bad. He as his attorney father only dealt with "beating the charge." Perhaps his was an extreme case. However, most criminals prefer not to get caught. If caught, they hope not to get punished, or at least punished minimally. Usually, they will do or say whatever it takes to avoid, delay or minimize their punishment.

One inmate from Chicago killed a policeman back in 1982, and his conviction was solid (NBC). Three Eye-witnesses, the murder weapon, being caught at the scene, and several other factors made it an open and shut case. However, the killer was soon able to get a lot of people, including several celebrities, on his side by a combination of outright lying and confusing the issue. He had been a winsome radio personality with a way with words. Of course, he used this to his advantage. Well meaning people all over the world are trying to get him released, or at least retried. What his supporters do not seem to realize is that anyone can reconstruct the facts (truth) to appear favorable to himself. A good talker can be very convincing, especially if people do not know the whole story. In this case, this person just made up his own story to look as though the police and prosecutors were at fault and he was just an innocent victim. However, there was an almost total disregard for the well established facts in the case. People should research the facts themselves, listen to both sides of the issue, and not just take one story as the truth, especially when the person presenting that viewpoint obviously has a vested interest in having his story accepted as truth.

The case of Michael Harris in North Carolina is another example of beating the system—almost (NBC) 20/20). He went on a homicidal rampage in the early 1980's, shooting nine people and killing four of them. After getting caught he said that he heard a voice from God telling him to do it. Whether his psychiatrist and his attorney really believed this convenient story is not certain, but they did convince the jury that he was insane at the time of the crime and, therefore, not guilty of murder. Nevertheless, he was sent to a state mental hospital, and at this writing (1999) the state has been able to keep him there by telling the judge that he is still insane and probably still dangerous. Although he still has not been released, his confinement in the state hospital is a much better deal than serving time in prison for murder or being on death row.

How easy for him to claim that he heard voices and is therefore insane and consequently not responsible for committing terrible crimes. Suddenly he is well again and wants out of the hospital, but the mentally ill do not just get well after a "psychotic episode." The truth of the matter is that he most likely never was insane. However, evidence suggests that he did have a history of violence, and although he has apparently not shown any aggressive or violent tendencies while in the hospital—he probably still is a violence risk. The law needs to be changed in North Carolina to do away with the "Not guilty by reason of insanity," and replaced with "Guilty—but insane," as some other states have. That way the perpetrator will go to the mental hospital until he or she gets well or is cured. Then he does his time.

Somewhat similar to the rehabilitation proponent's idea of the "cured criminal," religious people (usually evangelical Christians) believe that an inmate has been saved, converted, or "born again."

While there are no doubt some sincere religious conversions in prison, most are probably nothing more than tricky sociopaths playing a manipulative con game. Carla Faye Tucker from Texas played the "I'm a born-again Christian now" game very successfully, convincing many, even prison officials, of her sincerity. However, she was still eventually executed for the sadistic murder that she committed years earlier, in spite of the efforts of several Christian leaders, including Pat Robertson to get her off the hook (CNN),

Another successful con man is "Brother David" Berkowitz, the "son of Sam" serial killer (WABC, 1997). He has convinced many of his gullible supporters that he has been saved and is now a born-again Christian. He gets a lot of attention with this, and he has been on films that have had a wide distribution. Unfortunately, what his supporters do not deal with is the fact that Berkowitz continues to lie and has not come clean on his earlier lies and manipulations. To this day, he shows no real evidence of remorse for his crimes or concern for his victim's families (Singh, 2000). He is just one more example of why we need to stop these "prison ministries" and do-gooder visitations.

# SOCIOPATHS

## A. Who Are They?

WHAT IS A sociopath? This term is fairly new. The previous term psychopath was used for a long time until the American Psychological Association (APA) decided that the term sociopath was more accurate or descriptive. Although these people differ somewhat from person to person, certain characteristics seem to stand out across the board. First, there is the <u>total lack of conscience.</u> While sociopaths can tell someone that something is wrong, what they are doing is stating what they know others consider wrong, and not something they actually feel is wrong. They have little or no personal sense of right and wrong. They do whatever they consider beneficial to themselves and have no remorse for anything they have done. Of course, they do regret getting caught or punished, but not doing the wrong.

Another characteristic is the <u>total lack of empathy</u> or sympathy for anyone else. If people lose everything they have, suffer terrible emotional or physical pain, even lose their life, it will not bother a sociopath at all. Not only does the pain or misfortune of others not bother them, but many sociopaths actually enjoy it.

A third (and perhaps the most important) characteristic is their complete <u>inability to change or reform</u>. While they often show an amazing ability to convince others that they have changed or are going to change, it just does not happen. When we finally acknowledge this fact, we will stop wasting valuable time and money trying to rehabilitate or "fix" them, and hopefully we will stop releasing them from prison to continue preying on society. A serial killer may get better at luring potential victims, killing them, and not getting caught, but he will always be a danger.

A fourth characteristic is their unusual <u>ability to put up a front</u>. This is especially true of those who are physically and socially attractive, whether male of female. They are often very good liars and extremely adept at presenting themselves well when they feel that it is in their best interest to do so. Many people who should know better are taken in by them. This includes judges, physicians, psychologists, social workers, even parole officers and policemen, and others. Needless to say, if these trained people are misled, the average untrained person is even more easily duped.

A skilled sociopath can often fool a psychiatrist or psychologist. It happens all the time. Also, they often convince mental health persons that they are or were mentally ill or that they are now rehabilitated. Or they adopt whatever convenient diagnosis will help their cause. One physician who was poisoning people all over the country was interviewed by several psychiatrists for a job, and none of them picked up on the fact that there was even a problem (ABC News). Another example from a few years back was that of a female psychologist in California who was deceived by a sociopath. He ultimately killed four of his girlfriends, including her. Actually, training programs for psychiatrists, psychologists, and other therapists should go into a lot more detailed study of sociopaths and how they function, along with reviewing case histories where they have fooled therapists.

Most sociopaths are excellent con men or women. They easily make people like them or make people believe what they want them to believe. One attractive young woman from Texas lured different young men to her apartment where, after offering a back massage, she shot them—killing one. The body was dumped, and she stole his car and credit cards. After being sentenced to prison, she escaped along with another inmate. She had no trouble getting assistance from gullible young men while on the run (ABC). She dumped one and had a child by another. She married one who probably still visits her in prison to this day. Of course, she has convinced many people that she is just a poor, misunderstood angel who has never done anything wrong. Like the lady in Dallas who killed her children, she may very well weasel her way out of prison early.

Summary. Whether a traveling con man or a serial killer (or whatever), all sociopaths seem to have the following characteristics:

1. No conscience—Little or no concern for or sense of right and wrong or of society's norms and values.

2. No empathy—No care or concern for the feelings or problems of others.

3. Inability to change or reform—Contrary to what some might wish, they do not change or "get better" or become good citizens.

4. Excellent actors, liars and con men—When it suits their purposes, they can put up a good front—doing, acting, and saying all the "right" things, even seeming to be completely reformed. Very good actors, they can cry a flood of tears or present any front that will benefit them. They can even act mentally ill when it will get them acquitted or sent to a hospital instead of a prison

## B. How Do They Get That Way?

IF MOST CRIMINALS are sociopaths and these people are not reformable, who are they and how did they get that way? While there may be a genetic component affecting who will become a sociopath and how the condition will manifest itself (con man, serial killer, child molester, etc.), certain environmental factors (or the lack of them) tend to produce this type of character disorder rather consistently.

A brief review of the basic process of socialization is in order at this point. Many psychologists are aware of what follows. Unfortunately, some are not. When a child comes into the world into a nurturing family environment where he or she feels loved and accepted, the child develops a bond with the caregivers. This bond results in two very important things. First, by bonding with the caregivers, the child then identifies with them, and as a result of this identification both empathy and sympathy develop. With the right circumstances, these feelings are extended to others outside the family unit as well. He or she feels for others and, therefore, develops a concern for them as an extension of himself. On the other hand, never being accepted adequately and, therefore, never bonding nor developing any empathy for others, the sociopath grows up permanently lacking these normal human characteristics. Simply put—no acceptance or inadequate acceptance and nurturing causes no bonding, and no bonding creates people who have no concern for others—perhaps during the first two years of life. If it does not happen then, it probably will not or cannot ever happen, even with a better environment later.

When you see parents and their baby together in a healthy relationship, you observe their playing with the child, showing affection to him or her, talking with him, holding and caressing him, and you can see the positive effect all this has on the child. The bonding is starting, resulting in the child's developing the normal characteristics that make us human. Love, affection, caring, and kindness all have their roots here. What many of us do not often see is the reverse situation. What about the baby alone in the corner with no one to hold, love, caress, and talk to him: He is seldom changed, seldom picked up, and barely fed enough. He may even be slapped or otherwise abused for no reason. This child is not going to bond with any grown-ups. If he survives at all (and the chances are poor), he is not going to develop normal human characteristics or acquire accepted social values.

A continuing negative home environment will certainly add to the child's psychological deficits. One the other hand, changing the environment to a good or at least a better one after the first few bad months will probably not totally overcome the early negative effects. And some social worker or counselor is not going to show up later and give a teenager or adult all the positive strokes he needed as a child, thereby canceling all the negative effects of early childhood neglect and abuse.

What is more harmful, neglect or abuse? As stated earlier, severe neglect at an early age will prevent the bonding effect necessary for developing humanness and for internalizing social values. Add abuse to the neglect and we get hostility and a desire to strike out, against society in general, or possibly against women or children, or the targets may be a religious or racial group.

The case of Clifford Boggus comes to mind (CBS). He was executed recently in Texas for two murders committed during two separate robberies. People checked into his background and initially found very few problems. It seemed that he had a good family environment and was fairly well behaved as a child. However, further investigation revealed that he was adopted at around age two. One of his siblings in another state remembered that their birth mother seriously abused all of the children. Evidently, Clifford had been severely abused, even tortured, on a daily basis by his mother. Later when talking about brutally murdering the two store owners, he said that a hatred, hostility, and aggressiveness he did not know was there just came out and overwhelmed him. Apparently he forgot or repressed his early hatred and desire for revenge. Unfortunately, it came out later, resulting in his brutally killing two men. Was he a full-fledged sociopath? He later claimed to have had a religious conversion while in prison and to be sorry for what he had done. However, a conversion experience is impossible to verify, and people claiming one have been known to still be violent. Also, he did not seem to ever deal with his repressed violence.

The second result of proper bonding is that the child tends to internalize the beliefs and values of the "significant others." These values may or may not be desirable, but they come mostly from those bonded with, at least initially. (No bonding causes there to be no adequate internalization of any values.) The sociopath does what he or she wants to with little or no concern for what society or others think about it. They only concern themselves with what others think when it affects them personally, such as when society punishes some action they have done. But they do not have any internal sense of right and wrong or a conscience.

Some might object to this explanation of sociopathology and point out that Gary Gilmore, Ted Bundy, Jeffrey Dahmer, and others had siblings who did not turn out badly, but had this same non-accepting, non-bonding environment. However, several things can be said in answer. First, no two people in the same family ever have exactly the same social environment. Birth order and gender always have a strong effect. Also, one child can be accepted while the other is not. And, of course, a genetic component may very well make one sibling more predisposed to becoming a sociopath than another. Also, the so-called "good" sibling may not be all that good. It could be that their offenses either were not as severe or just did not come to the attention of society or the authorities.

A well-known psychiatrist who studied Arthur Shawcross said that many violent criminals suffered severe head injuries during childhood (Wilson). Others have made the same observations; therefore, head injuries should no doubt be taken into consideration as a possible contributing factor—at least in some cases. However, many violent and dangerous people have not had head injuries, and most people who have had head injuries do not become violent or dangerous. Therefore, while head injuries may contribute a little to undesirable behavior in some cases and a lot in other cases, it probably is not a significant factor in most cases.

Many times it is relatively easy to see the causes of someone becoming violent or anti-social. Interviewing the person, the family, friends, and reviewing his life history shows early and severe neglect and often abuse as well. It becomes very clear how he or she became the way he or she is. How could he be any different? For instance, when one learns that the father seriously abused both the children and the mother, and there was little or no nurturing or bonding—it is clear what happened. On the other hand, there are cases that are not so obvious—at least not on the surface. One may investigate a career criminal or even a serial killer, and his parents seem to always have been stable, caring and nurturing individuals. The temptation is to assume that the parents and other caregivers are not responsible for the problem, or even contributors to it. They may be pillars of the community—doctors, lawyers, teachers, businessmen, ministers, and others who are well liked and respected. There is little similarity to the violent, abusive and dysfunctional parents we are sure caused other children's problems. But when one digs deeper, the same neglect, lack of nurturing, and possible abuse combined with little or no bonding was often there all along. And neglect does not have to be material. A child can grow up well-fed, well-clothed, with plenty of money and other material things and still be psychologically neglected, which is the most harmful type of neglect. The Menendez brothers, who were tried for killing their parents in the 1990's were apparently an example of this. They had everything they wanted: clothes, money, parties, travel, and other material things; but evidently they never got what they needed: love, affection, nurturing, and a close and caring family.

Jeffrey Dahmer's father presented himself well on television, seeming to be a normal man. Many thought that surely Jeffrey must have had a brain injury or a genetic defect that caused him to do the things he did. What was not so evident was the extreme neglect he experienced from birth. The mother left him and his father when he was still a young teenager. Evidently, she did not even say goodbye. Later, while Jeffrey was still in high school, the father left him as well. Apparently, he did not say goodbye either. This indicates a family with no bonding. Also, the father seemingly did not notice that Jeffrey was torturing, killing, and dismembering small animals while growing up.

Intelligent, stable, caring, kind, and nurturing parents do not produce a Jeffrey Dahmer. Someone who has experienced love and kindness while growing up does not torture, kill, mutilate, abuse and cannibalize people. Unfortunately, as adults these sociopaths are not "fixable."

Some people have pointed out that Kenneth Allen McDuff, and others like him, were not abused or neglected as children (Lavergne). Instead, they were spoiled and overindulged. Kenneth's mother consistently defended him to everyone regardless of what wrong he did. They also point out that none of the other siblings became sadistic serial killers. This seeming contradiction is not, however, too hard to answer. While it may be true that Kenneth Allen McDuff was overindulged with material things even into adulthood, it seems that he was indeed neglected emotionally, if not materially. Neighbors stated that the mother, like other similar parents, was domineering, controlling, and totally in denial of reality (Lavergne).

Abuse, like neglect, does not have to be physical. Psychological abuse can also be devastating, especially when combined with emotional neglect. Even if the child has adequate or an abundance of material things, that is not enough for proper psychological development. As already stated, the young child must experience love, affection, attention, and nurturing in order to psychologically bond with the caregiver. Without bonding the child will never develop empathy or concern for the parent, nor anyone else. Also, when the child perceives that the parent shows concern for others, he will learn to extend these feelings to others as well. On the other hand, if he does not observe the parent showing any concern for others, he will not learn any care or concern either. Also, when a parent always defends the child no matter how obviously in the wrong he is, he will grow up thinking that other's rights and feelings do not matter, and that any wrong he does is perfectly all right. While a materially overindulged child who was also psychologically abused and neglected may show some characteristics that are somewhat different from many other sociopaths, in most ways they are essentially the same.

What about the idea that many sociopaths, including serial killers, have brothers, sisters and other relatives who are seemingly perfectly normal (normal being defined as basically law abiding, productive and well adjusted). This difference among siblings is probably due to a somewhat different environment. However, it is seldom researched adequately. And in other instances that were looked into, researchers found that they too were violent, criminal, or dysfunctional, even though they were not serial killers and did not come to the attention of the public.

## C. The Futility of Trying to Treat Them (Sociopaths)

WHEN I FIRST went to work for the Tennessee Department of Corrections, I found that the employees were divided into broad categories: Treatment and Security. The treatment people, mostly educated in the social sciences such as psychology, sociology, social work, etc., were primarily concerned with programs such as counseling, visitation, and sports to work toward the rehabilitation of the inmates. The security people, often not college graduates, were mainly concerned with preventing escapes and running or controlling the prisons.

Often the treatment people were confirmed believers in rehabilitation, at least when they first started work and had not yet met the hard facts of reality. On the other hand, most of the security people, not being indoctrinated into the latest social theory or fad, had fewer illusions about criminals and deviants ever becoming good people. There seemed to be a silent disagreement between these two groups within the prison system. Gradually I came to see that the security people actually had a more accurate and realistic opinion concerning the type of people we had in prison.

If misguided do-gooders had not come up with the idea of rehabilitation in the first place, we would not even have a treatment department or program. This idea is relatively new—less than 200 years old. Some countries, more enlightened in this area, such as Japan do not even buy into the concept.

Often we hear talk about the need for more rehabilitation, and one justification is that since most bad or dangerous people will eventually be released from prison, we therefore need to "fix" them so they will no longer be dangerous or harmful when they are let out. Of course, this is faulty reasoning. First, they cannot be fixed and they definitely will be at least potentially dangerous when they are released. Trying to fix the "unfixable" is not the solution. The intelligent solution is not to release them. We need to seriously rethink parole, probation, bond, and short sentences for potentially dangerous people. For instance, ten years in prison for someone who has murdered a child is absurd.

Sometimes we hear stories about reformed gangsters, gang members, jewel thieves, and others who seem to have made a big change in their lives. Now they are helping law enforcement. Some have a religious component to their "change of heart," and others do not. However, we need to look seriously at these cases when we are tempted to use them as examples of rehabilitation. First, have they really changed that much, or have they just convinced us that they have changed? Second, were they just rebellious young people who were not actually sociopathic, and the so-called change, if it existed, was just one of becoming a little less rebellious? Cruel and sadistic people do not change. They may become less active and aggressive as they get older, but that is mostly due to reduced energy, and not because of any real change in psychological orientation.

Most people working in corrections are well acquainted with the revolving door syndrome. They see a prisoner being released by parole, probation, sentence completion, or whatever. Then in a relatively short time they see him coming back again. In all too many cases this happens over and over again—hence the term "revolving door." These people never change, never get better, but we still continue releasing them to prey on society over and over again. Most of the few who do not return to prison have probably moved to another state or just become more skilled at not being caught, prosecuted, or convicted.

One misguided visitor to Brushy Mountain Prison was trying to make the case for not giving murderers long prison sentences. His rationale was that most murderers were not repeat offenders and, therefore, posed no continuing threat to society, so there was no point in keeping them locked up very long. I found this belief to be fairly widespread among rehabilitation advocates. Actually, most murderers are aggressive and violent people whether or not they actually continue killing after being released, but many of them do.[7]

Someday, when we have the technology to accurately identify violence-prone people and potential criminals (See Chapter IV), we will need to either "cure" them or remove them from society in advance. At the present time we are not doing a very good job of identifying them, although we could do a lot better, but we certainly cannot cure them. However, if the desire is there, we may someday be able to both identify and cure potentially problematical people before they do negative things. Of course, this would be better for both them and for society. Unfortunately, today (1999) we do not have the ability to do it. And, counseling, therapy, and treatment do not do it.

How can you tell when a sexual sociopath, rapist or gang member is rehabilitated? You cannot. The method we have tried to use is primarily based on what the client tells us. The problem is that sociopathic offenders are often infinitely smarter than their psychologists or counselors. They soon learn what is in their best interest to say and how to act in such a way so as to give the illusion of rehabilitation. But a counselor cannot go by that. We have been wrong far too many times. Sadistic and violent offenders are almost certain to re-offend. And just because someone acted properly while locked up does not mean he will be a good citizen when released.

There are a few cases when someone who has been rebellious seems to show a change for the better. However, these people are usually not violent or sexual offenders, and any change is mostly due to the person's own reorientation—not due to some externally applied counseling or therapy. The person has to have a conscience, the desire to change, and the motivation to change—three things sociopaths do not have.

There was a program, on television (9-21-99) about Buford Furrow, the man who shot the children at the Jewish community center and also killed the Filipino mailman in California. It seems that in the past he had told several people many times that he eventually would do something violent. Friends, acquaintances, law enforcement people, including the deputy who previously arrested him, and mental health workers all knew about his ultimate intentions. Nevertheless, both the Washington State judge and the prosecutor, after making absolutely no effort to find out what kind of person they were dealing with, decided to set him free. Of course, we see what happened.

The interviewer who was questioning the prison official about what was done in Furrow's case did not get very far. Although the official tried to explain or excuse not prosecuting Furrow, he did not seem to have a clue about what kind of person they were dealing with, or why they should have made an effort to find out. Releasing him is just another example of incompetent people running our prisons and functioning as judges. Even though dangerous people are set free all the time, we never seem to learn. Supposedly there was recent legislation to prevent the easy release of dangerous people. Seemingly, it did not do much good.

Buford Furrow's case is an example of an obviously dangerous mentally ill person. He may or may not also be a sociopath, but he is not so mentally ill that he does not know what he is doing, nor should he be excused from paying the consequences.

Although most criminals are probably sociopathic, as previously stated, this does not explain all anti-social behavior. There are other types of people who get into trouble with the law or do inappropriate or violent things. For instance, there are people with a lot of repressed rage or hostility, and they certainly can become abusive or violent at the slightest real or imagined provocation. This can result in child abuse, spousal abuse, criminal assault or even murder, even though these people are often technically law abiding citizens, and not criminals. They are often hard working, very honest, and seemingly good citizens in every other respect. It is usually a big surprise when they end up killing someone or doing some other violent thing. Probably, many cases of road rage are examples of this type of person.

I once knew a man named Ernest (not his real name), who was an excellent example of this. He was tall, nice looking, well groomed, and one of the most polite persons I have ever met—to the point of overdoing it. He was also a good citizen in every respect. An excellent businessman, electrician, and auto mechanic, he already had accumulated a small fortune while only in is early twenties. But what a temper! He was totally unpredictable. Everything could be going just fine, but if anyone disagreed with him about the smallest or most insignificant thing, or confronted him in any way, he would fly into an uncontrollable rage like a madman. He would try to kill you over nothing. Once, he went after a man with a hammer over some disagreement about football. After a few similar incidents, I discontinued our friendship. Although he would frequently call me for us to meet and do something, I was always too busy or otherwise unavailable. I did not want him to injure or kill me over something irrelevant, or for me to have to hurt him in self-defense. He was totally unpredictable, so there was no way to avoid setting him off. Later on I learned that, unlike sociopaths, these rage driven people can sometimes be treated, if they are self-motivated to change.

Usually, little or nothing is done to protect the public from potentially dangerous people, whether mentally ill, sociopathic (and they are not the same), or whatever. Officials knew about John Hinkley and did virtually nothing until he shot the president and others. Law enforcement people knew the man who shot the two Capitol guards in 1998, and even the CIA has a video-taped interview with him. However, nothing was done. Both of these people should have been institutionalized, and they probably would have been 30 or more years ago—until we decided to let most people out of mental hospitals, and made it much more difficult to commit anyone. We certainly have overdone this deinstitutionalization.

The case in Nevada of the young man from California who killed a little black girl in a casino while his friend looked on, walked away, and did nothing, might have been a little harder to predict. His teachers and others said that he was a polite, well-behaved student. Perhaps! But the telltale signs were probably there all along, if the right people only knew what to look for. But, of course, it would not have done any good, since we no longer lock up mentally ill people in advance or for very long, and very often not even after they have actually done something to show that they need it.

Cary Steiner, who killed the four women in Yosemite National Park in 1999, basically had gotten away with killing the first three (Smith, 1999). It seems that the authorities had no clue about him until he decapitated the fourth person. Maybe they did not look hard enough, or people who knew some things about him did not speak up. It appears that in the past he had told friends about considering killing all his coworkers in a mass killing. They knew he had said that, and so did the place where he was supposed to go for counseling. Also, the idea that Steiner had felt a compulsion to kill women from an early age, but had only acted on it in his late 30's is highly improbable. What is more likely is that he had been killing people for years, but just had not been caught yet. The manner in which he talked his way into the three women's room, tricked them into letting him tie them up before killing them, and then led the authorities on a false trail by dropping one of their wallets off in a nearby town, indicates a highly experienced and successful sexually sadistic serial killer. As I will suggest in Chapter IV, we may someday have the technology to take someone like Steiner, strap him to a table, hook electrodes to specific parts of his brain, and thereby find out what type of person he is, what he is capable of doing, and specifically what he has done in the past.

In June 2000 there was a program on television about a 13-year-old-boy waiting to be tried for a murder committed when he was 11 years old. They showed the old familiar debate between the two sides. On one hand, the defense maintained that he was too young to fully understand what he had done, and therefore he should neither be held fully accountable nor tried as an adult. Since most six year-olds know it is wrong to kill people, that does not seem to be a realistic point of view. And the mother appeared totally unaware that she could have contributed in any way to her son's being a sociopath. She thought that he needed help via counseling—not punishment or confinement.

What nobody seemed to realize, unfortunately, is that this child is most likely a sociopath and already beyond reform. He just is not going to "turn good," or be "fixed" by counseling and therapy. As stated earlier, this type of person is already set in their ways at a very early age—probably before age two. We need to stop producing these violent and dangerous people in the first place, not try to fix them after they have done something wrong at age 10, 12, 14 or whenever. Unfortunately, the only thing that can be done with this child and others like him is to lock him up for the protection of society. While counseling might help him adjust to prison, nothing will ever make him not potentially dangerous if and when he gets out.

Summary: What we need to do at the present time is this: We need to do a much better job of identifying the home and other environments that produce sociopaths and deviant people in the first place. Children should be removed early. Defective parents should probably be sterilized and prevented from adopting. When a psychopathic killer or sexual offender is convicted, it should be for life—no exceptions. And until we can actually do it, we need to forget about rehabilitation.

# DO-GOODERS

## A. Every Prison Has Them

WHEN I TRANSFERRED to Brushy Mountain Prison as a school-teacher from the Knoxville work release program, I met some very strange people. Volumes of these people would come to the prison on a regular basis to work with inmates through the treatment program. They did visitation, counseled, brought presents, wrote letters, and also helped the inmates get new trials, probation and other types of release. Not infrequently some of the women visitors would become romantically involved with inmates, occasionally resulting in marriages.

There seem to be a lot of these people. They are drawn to prisons and prisoners like bugs to a light or metal flakes to a magnet. Often they seek out the very worst inmates—the serial killers, brutal murderers, and child rapists. Later on I learned that prisons everywhere in the United States were plagued by these do-gooders. Some just show up at the institutions. Some are relatives. Others start out as attorneys, reporters, social workers, or missionaries.

Some of these people claim just to be interested in befriending and helping a variety of inmates. Others concentrate on only one or two. Some are writers or social scientists interested in understanding or writing about inmates in general, or they may be interested in specific types—such as serial killers. The true reason is probably that they are interested and fascinated with these people because they identify with them—at least subconsciously.

## B. What Makes a Do-Gooder?

WHY WOULD SEEMINGLY normal people take an obsessive interest in incorrigible sociopathic inmates? At first it appears quite unusual until one meets, gets to know them, and finds out the life histories of some of these do-gooders. After checking out several of them, one sees a pattern emerge just as it does for sociopaths. These people are drawn to sociopaths primarily because they identify with them. The sociopath represents what they would like to be but have not totally become.

Most zealots trying to help inmates were somewhat alienated from their family, schools, and friends, for at least part of their formative years. They often feel rejected and misunderstood by them. They feel like rebelling, but they cannot quite bring themselves to do it—at least not to the extent the inmates have. They do admire and identify with those who have done it, and they feel sorry for them and want to help them if they are in trouble or have problems.

These people have a mental fixation combining an obsession and identification with the inmates, along with a type of denial of what they are really like and the terrible things they have done. Both James Earl Ray (for a while) and Henry Lee Lucas acquired girlfriends who were totally convinced of their innocence in spite of overwhelming evidence of their guilt Other girlfriends are aware of the crimes their inmate friends have done, but seemingly do not care. Most normal people are totally baffled by this. For instance, how could anyone believe that someone who had sexually abused, tortured and murdered ten or more children was a good guy and someone to be friends with and help? There are many good people in the world who need and deserve both help and friendship, but the do-gooder types usually show no interest or concern for them. They would rather spend their time, effort, and money on those who do not deserve it. This is not unusual for prison do-gooders. There was a convicted murderer at Brushy Mountain Prison in Tennessee who had over 15 people coming to see him from Oak Ridge on a regular basis. On their way there they passed the home of the widow and children of his victim every time they came to the prison. They never wrote them, came to see them, or gave them any assistance of any type. It is like the victims did not matter. Only the killer was important, which seems backwards in a civilized society (world, etc.). Of course, do-gooders seldom identify with victims.

## C. Keeping Them Away

MANY OF THE security people that I have talked with over the years, from the guards on up to the wardens, considered these do-gooders to be a nuisance, something useless that just had to be endured. On the other hand, the treatment people often had different opinions among themselves. Some thought these visitors were a positive influence, some considered them an annoyance, and others did not seem to have any opinion whatsoever.

Many employees at prisons where I have worked wondered why people not related to the inmates would seek them out as pen pals or people to visit. When I asked the visitors what their motivation was, they would often say that they were interested in helping people. However, when I would ask them why they did not help the poor and the disabled instead of these people who did not seem to need or deserve it, their answer was usually unclear or evasive. In most cases I am sure they were not fully aware of the true reasons.

Over a period of time, by both observing and talking with these correspondents and visitors, I have become convinced that their primary reason for seeking out inmates is a fascination with them based on either admiration for or identification with them—not on any desire to help people or do good.

Often these people try to help the inmates get released, sometimes successfully. They see the prison system as the enemy—at least to some extent. Some go a little further. There are cases on record, from the days of Bonnie and Clyde to the present, of these people actually helping inmates escape from prison. Others, like James Earl Ray's wife, gradually get fed up with these manipulative con men and quit trying to help them or even write to them.

Since one universal characteristic of sociopaths is to use and manipulate people, inmates are often only too eager to accept the friendship of these prison groupies. As long as they feel that they can gain something from the association, the inmates may continue the relationship indefinitely, even after release from prison. However, if they can no longer benefit from the association or they find someone more useful, they often drop the "friend" completely. There are even cases where they have actually murdered these no longer useful do-gooders.

What do the inmates think of these people? Some will not have anything to do with them. However, many inmates like the attention and the fact that they can get a lot of help and material goods from them—books, stationary items, and even money. On the other hand, I have heard many inmates say that they think these people are foolish and someone to be used and taken advantage of. Of course, there are a few prisoners who seem to really appreciate this attention, but even they often say that they do not understand it. Those few inmates who seem to truly appreciate them are usually non-violent, non-sociopathic types.

These prison do-gooders come in two basic types: the non-religious types who are interested in providing assistance and association and others who basically are in interested in providing religious services—Catholic, Jewish, Muslim, or whatever.

Often evangelical Christians feel they have a mission to bring the gospel message to even the worst of the prisoners. Actually, the New Testament admonition to take the gospel message to the entire world does not say anything about going into prisons. Also, the idea about visiting those in prison applies to fellow Christians who have been locked up for the faith, not to rapists, killers, and criminals.

Since sociopaths do not have a conscience and will not develop one, they are not going to have any authentic remorse or make any drastic change—although they can do an excellent job of faking it when it suits their purposes. I recall one inmate who supposedly was "born again," and even became a preacher. When he completed his sentence, on the way out of prison he threw his Bible into the trash can, cursed at those seeing him off, and gave them an obscene gesture. He got a lot of benefits by being "saved," but it did not last past the prison door. All the preachers and church workers who come to the prison would be well advised to put their effort where it will have results.

How can we keep these people away from jails and prisons? It is going to be hard to do because the humanitarian visitors think they have the right to visit and the religious ones believe they have a mission or a God-given mandate. Actually, there probably should be a national policy to keep most of these visitors out. They are a nuisance for the employees and serve no useful purpose. These people need to satisfy their fascination and identification with sociopaths in some other way. If and when we actually become able to reform criminals, it will be through medicine—not with untrained visitors.

One of the two Alabama inmates who killed a gay acquaintance now claims that God forgave him. However, even in the Christian tradition, remorse and repentance are essential aspects for forgiveness. A trite insincere "I'm sorry" does not mean anything when the killer still justifies his crime.

There is another type of do-gooder. They may not be trying to "save" or even help prisoners directly. They may not visit prisons or jails, and often do not even work in this area. Some of what these people do is probably good. As we discuss in Chapter V, there are, even to this day, cruel and inhumane prisons and jails. Inmates are unnecessarily abused, and in some places female prisoners are still being sexually harassed and abused. So it is good that there are some who are still willing to speak up and do something. Ironically, the worst inmates are often the ones who receive the most benign treatment. One serial killer who kidnapped, tortured, murdered, and dismembered dozens of girls and women now has a cushy job being in charge of the computers and electrical systems at a large prison. Clearly inappropriate! If we are not going to execute people like him, we should at least confine them for 23 hours per day—with no benefits. There may be some things that do-gooders need to do, but they do not need to be helping people like this.

# BRAIN MAPPING, GENETICS, AND DNA BANKS

## A. Brain Mapping

RECENTLY THERE HAVE been some advances in what is called brain mapping (ICBM). Specific areas of the brain can be identified that are responsible for specific problems or behaviors. We are not there yet, but it seems probable that in the future we may be able to locate where hostility, aggressiveness, and other negative tendencies are located in the brain. We may be able to "map" or locate the specific areas in the brain that make the serial killer, rapist, thief, child molester, or whatever. Hopefully, we could know in advance exactly who has the tendency or inclination to do these and other undesirable anti-social things. Perhaps, at that point we could treat the potential problem or possibly remove the person from society. This would make infinitely more sense than waiting until there were several victims before dealing with the problem.

Since talking treatments have traditionally had little or no effect on sociopathic personalities, we will need a new approach. After mapping the client's brain and locating where the problem causing areas are, step two would be to surgically, chemically, or electrically alter them to minimize their problem-causing potential. Then true reform may actually be possible.

If we are going to do any treatment at all, it certainly makes a lot more sense to "treat" or "cure" a potentially harmful person in advance than to do it after he has done something terrible. Also, it would be much better for the potential victim never to have to suffer the results of a crime, such as being harmed or killed. Of course, the potential perpetrator would not have to be punished either. No doubt it will be a long time before society will accept the idea of changing people's brains, minds, or personalities, but who can argue with the idea of eliminating or at least minimizing characteristics such as cruelty and hostility, as long as the positive aspects of personality such as love and kindness are not harmed. What harm would there be if we eliminated hatred and cruelty altogether.

## B. Genetics

ANOTHER AREA TO be investigated is genetics. There are, no doubt, genetic components of aggressiveness, hostility, and violence in at least some cases, but other factors help create the sociopath or criminal. Locating, and possibly altering, these genes or the results of them, would have a similar advantage to brain mapping. But what does one do once one knows about potentially harmful genes. While it might not be desirable to change the genes themselves, it might be possible to affect those parts of the brain the gene has influenced negatively.

There are no doubt some types of schizophrenia, autism, and other mental conditions that cause problem behaviors—even violence. As both a social worker and a psychiatric aide, I have worked with children and adults who were very violence prone. Some were violent almost continuously and toward almost everyone, while others were only violent on occasion and only toward certain individuals.

These people are not sociopathic. They probably have a chemical imbalance or some structural injury or abnormality. Still, brain mapping or genetic mapping probably can assist in identifying the conditions and possibly improving them as well.

Also people exist who are at least verbally aggressive with a "short fuse," people who get angry easily, with slight or no provocation. Some limit their attacks to verbal assaults, while others can be more physical. If they are not otherwise mentally ill or sociopathic, these people can and do learn either to control or to direct their anger, even if not eliminating it. However, in a "culture of violence" where children are taught "not to take anything" from anybody and to "standup for yourself," these people may get into trouble (Rhodes, 1999,[8] although they are not technically criminals. They may assault, beat up, or even kill someone who insults them, challenges them, or becomes competition for their girlfriend.

Recently (November, 1999) one woman shot and killed another in what appears to have been a road rage incident in Alabama. Evidently, the first woman cut off the other on the freeway, intentionally or not. The second woman then started tailgating the first one, until they both stopped at an intersection. The first one then got out of her car and walked back to the other car, when the second woman pulled out her gun and shot and killed her. It seems that neither woman had any criminal record or history of violence. However, this is the type of thing latent hostility can lead to, especially now that many are carrying guns in some places.

## C. The Use of DNA Banks

OUR DNA OR genetic makeup determines almost everything about us; our hair and eye color, our height and weight and even what hereditary diseases we are susceptible to are all determined by our DNA makeup. Like fingerprints, no two people have ever been found to have the exact same prints.

The idea of having DNA banks has already met with opposition. Some people feel that this would be a violation of people's rights. However, DNA banks would be as useful as fingerprints. DNA has already been used in establishing both guilt and innocence in several crimes. However, there can be additional uses for DNA banks. Eventually, we may be able to pinpoint potential behaviors through DNA identification. We could then know who actually did something by identifying the DNA, and also who might be inclined toward certain behaviors by identifying specific genes.

Since rehabilitation is basically a myth, and we need to eliminate the entire concept, brain mapping and genetic mapping may give us the tools to truly change people for the better.

There are thousands of examples of how our belief in rehabilitation continues to cause us to release violent and dangerous people. A woman from New York was recently released from prison after serving only 15 years of a 25-year-to-life sentence for murder. She took her daughter into the rest room of a restaurant and beat her to death for spilling food. Now, this supposedly rehabilitated person is going to be teaching parenting skills to other abusive women, yet her only parenting ended in her daughter's death.

Why discuss brain mapping, genetics and DNA banks in a book about rehabilitation, or actually its non-existence? The reason is that what we usually think of as rehabilitation just does not exist. We cannot change people for the better with counseling or other programs. Therefore, if we are ever going to do it, it will be with one of these ideas.

# V

# MISCELLANEOUS THOUGHTS

## A. Meanness, Cruelty, and Sadism

MEANNESS, CRUELTY, AND sadism are probably just different degrees of the same thing. Small children can often be very cruel to others. Frequently, the victims are either different or just weaker and unwilling or unable to defend themselves. Sometimes meanness is in retaliation for something the victim may actually or supposedly have done. Other times the enjoyment of seeing someone or something suffer is the only known motivator. I recall some young children torturing grasshoppers and toads by pulling off their legs, until I suggested that this was not proper. I do not believe that they were taught to do this, although they may have observed other children doing it. They just decided it would be fun to mistreat smaller helpless creatures who could neither escape nor defend themselves.

In March of 1997, in Fairfield, Iowa two 18-year-olds broke into an animal shelter and killed 16 cats with baseball bats (Jewel, 1997, p.154).[4] Needless cruelty to cats and dogs is still prevalent in this country. One man made the statement that they were "just cats." But we need to remember that Jeffrey Dahmer, and others like him, also killed "just animals," until he graduated to killing and eating humans (WABC). The truth of the matter is that violence and sadism are negative and undesirable characteristics, regardless of who or what the victims are. Laws, of course, are helpful in reducing animal cruelty, but the most effective thing is education. And while it may be true that not all of those who are cruel toward animals are also or will become cruel to humans, the potential is there. Many serial killers have been cruel to animals in their past (WABC)[4] Probably all schools have bullies, and possibly quite a few people have been bullies themselves at one time or another. Therefore, the potential for meanness or cruelty toward others may be a latent characteristic in most people, if not actively discouraged.

Teachers, coaches and military drill instructors can often be cruel or sadistic. Often, they excuse it, at least to themselves, as either necessary or in some way beneficial to the victims. Recently, a former policeman made a speech on television (NBC)[1] primarily discussing the doing away with the Miranda warning to suspects. He did make some interesting side comments in his talk. In one he said that he had been a policeman himself for about 40 years, that he liked policemen and both supported and admired them and the work they did. However, he did stress very strongly that it was absolutely necessary that they be regulated and controlled. Any time the police (or the military) are not answerable to anyone but themselves, abuses will tend to occur. What happened a few years ago in Argentina, Chile, and other similar places are excellent examples of this. The police and the military kidnapped, tortured, raped, and murdered thousands of suspected subversives, without any due process or humanitarian guidelines whatsoever. Some victims may have been guilty of something, perhaps having the wrong political beliefs. Many, however, were probably guilty of nothing. When things returned to more normal conditions, very little was done to punish the perpetrators. The preceding are two examples of what can happen when there is not control over police or military authorities, no accountability, and no policy of due process.

Much has been made of the atrocities committed in Cambodia on their own people, and more recently in Bosnia and Korsovo by the Serbs, and in Africa by various factions. Both the Japanese and the Germans were notorious for mistreating and killing both prisoners and civilians during the Second World War. What we seldom talk about is that the American military (and police) can be just as cruel, brutal, and inhuman as anyone else. Our conquest of the Philippine Islands was as brutal and savage on both sides as any war known in the history of mankind. Also, the conduct of our military during the war in Viet Nam had no resemblance to what a humanitarian and democratic country would do. We totally ignored the Geneva Convention's rules of war. From the top generals down to the foot soldiers, there was a policy of torturing and murdering prisoners of war as well as mistreating civilians, including beating, raping, and murdering them (Elliot, 1996). The very few who were ever convicted of doing these things invariable had their sentences cancelled or reduced. Of course, most were never punished. Often those who objected or showed any reservations about the brutality were labeled as cowardly, unmanly, or even as unloyal or traitors. Actually, many who opposed the war, or at least the conduct of it, in Viet Nam believed that it was the military people themselves who were the traitors to both humanity and democracy, by becoming as bad or even worse than those they were fighting against. Concepts such as right and wrong disappeared altogether, and the only important values became winning, along with an "us" and "them" mentality, a warped viewpoint also all too common in police departments.

Recently, the murder of a couple hundred civilians in Korea in 1950 came to light, demonstrating that the My Lai incident and others like it were not limited to Viet Nam or any particular nation (CBS). Some in the military tried to convince the public that these atrocities were unusual aberrations, and not the norm. Actually, in Viet Nam both torture and murder were the norm (Elliot).

Recently, a former soldier who spoke out against My Lai was invited to speak at two of the military academies (CBS-NBC). He was well received by both students and officers. However, this is a very new attitude. For almost 30 years, the top brass considered him a troublemaker, if not an outright traitor—all because he objected to and spoke out against the torture and murder that went on in Viet Nam.

Often military atrocities seem far away; however, when civilians kill people at home, it seems to be more shocking. The Luby's massacre in Killeen, Texas by George Hennard in October1991 is one of the worst mass murders in recent history. I happened to be only one block away at the time it happened. In fact, since I often had eaten lunch there, it was just luck that I was not present at the time. In the past few years there have been many mass killings—one in Atlanta and several school shootings. In some ways they are similar, and in other ways they are each unique.

There are several differences between mass murderers and serial killers. Mass murders are often done with little or no concern for the killer's own safety. Murderers often do not consider escape, intentionally take their own life, or put themselves in a position where they can or will be killed. Also, these incidents are usually hostility and revenge motivated, not sexually and hostility motivated as are serial killings. And (sexually sadistic) serial killers usually try to commit their crimes in secret, where they can avoid detection. And while revenge and hostility are often involved as well, it is the sexual component that distinguishes them from most mass murderers. They find sexual enjoyment in dominating, terrorizing, and killing their victims. But they usually do not want to be caught or punished themselves. Another difference is that often mass murderers seem to be mentally ill (insane). Hennard obviously was. However, serial killers such as Ted Bundy are usually not. They are usually sociopaths, which is another thing.

While the capacity to mistreat other humans, or animals, is probably innate, people can learn either to be cruel or not to be cruel, depending on how they are socialized (Rhodes, 1999).[8] On the other hand, soldiers, policemen, and guards who behave properly in society in general can easily slip into cruelty and even sadism toward their "enemies" when they come to believe that it is proper or even just acceptable (Rhodes). Most of the soldiers who committed rape and murder in Viet Nam did not continue committing these crimes after their return to society, where these crimes would not be tolerated. A few did. The infamous Shawcross from New York claimed to have started killing women in Viet Nam (Wilson, 1995, p. 336).

In the Temple, Texas area in 1999, only a few months apart, two women were murdered by young men less than 20 years old. Both homicides were thrill or sexually sadistic killings. Since both killers were caught and sentenced to prison, they probably will not become serial killers unless they are released, as many dangerous people are. By definition, serial killers are successful killers. If they are caught and locked up the first time, that may be the end of it. But thrill killers who enjoy killing may continue for a very long time, unless they are stopped.

One victim was a reporter who was killed in her own apartment by a young man who was caught before he could get away. The other victim had been successful in social services. Her killer was apprehended later while using her credit cards. Some people including reporters and attorneys who should know better expressed surprise that neither young man showed any remorse. Many people just do not understand that sexual sadists, people who enjoy torturing and killing for the fun of it, are not going to feel any remorse. If they do express any, it is invariable insincere and for the purpose of getting supporters for their cause. One might possibly get into a fist fight with his brother-in-law, accidentally kill him, and then feel remorse; but one who plans a murder, enjoys it, then brags about it to his friends, is not going to feel remorse when he is caught. He is proud of what he did, and surely will do it again if he has the opportunity to do so. Sociopaths might fake remorse to manipulate people into siding with them and helping them out, and there may be some regret for being caught or punished, but there is not going to be any genuine remorse for the victims or what was done.

Most normal people just cannot comprehend how someone could plan a murder, torture and rape the victim, then mutilate the body, and thoroughly enjoying the entire process. Thrill killers, however, are totally different from most of us. They do not have the same feelings for others and the same sense of right and wrong that most people do. Therefore, to try and understand them by assuming that they are motivated in any way like most of us can only lead to incorrect conclusions. One young lady, in her early twenties, after interviewing several inmates, was expressing her opinions about crime and its causes on television (NBC). She was basing almost all of what she thought on what the inmates themselves told her, and it soon became apparent that she had almost no insight whatsoever into crime or criminals. In the first place, very few inmates have any insight into the causes of crime themselves, so they could not be helpful even if they wanted to. Ted Bundy surely did not (Michard, 1993).[5] Others like him did not either. Also, even if criminals did have some understanding, very few of them will be truthful about it.

Author James Stewart said on television (1999), while discussing one of his books (*Blind Eye*), that sociopaths cannot be helped, changed, or rehabilitated by any medication or therapy that we presently know about. And contrary to what misguided do-gooders believe, he is essentially accurate. A serial killer does what he does because he enjoys killing people, and he does not care about the victims. John Douglas, another author who had done extensive work with serial killers, has also said that he has never encountered a serial killer who had a loving, caring, stable early childhood (1995, Ch. 18). Of course, many people have less than a perfect or even desirable early childhood, and seemingly turn out all right (Rhodes). However, a seriously bad childhood, with a lot of neglect and abuse, usually produces maladjusted and dysfunctional people who are often sociopathic.

Because these people never received the attention and affection that all of us need in order to grow up normally, they lack the qualities that make us human. Love, affection, concern, and understanding are characteristics that they do not have, and although they can often present a good outward personality or front, these human qualities just are not there. These qualities, and the ability to have them, develop very early in life (George, 1995, Ch. VI). They can, no doubt, be reinforced or minimized, depending upon subsequent experiences while growing up, but the early effect, if negative, probably can never be overcome totally.

An acquaintance of mine adopted two children a boy and a girl. Evidently, they had been severely neglected and abused, first by their natural parents, then later by different foster homes. These children were totally unreceptive to any overtures of friendship or affection by their newly adoptive parents. As time went on, they became more unmanageable. In fact, the boy became quite violent, aggressive, and a real danger to the adoptive parents. Ultimately, he had to be institutionalized for the parents' own safety. Too late it became apparent that they had not been given a detailed and accurate history of these children's early life. In fact, many things had been deliberately hidden from the adoptive parents. The damage to these children was already done, and no doubt was irreversible by the time they were adopted. No amount of belated love, caring and nurturing did any good. Other similar cases abound. One just cannot apply the proper parenting later in his life that a child should have received at an early age and expect it to do much good. Unfortunately, belated care just does not work.

Primitive tribes often act quite cruelly toward other tribes, especially in warfare. Genocide, infanticide, and torture are often the norm (Rhodes, 1999, Ch 18). And this behavior is very similar to what one finds in inner city and other gangs, where outsiders are considered enemies not worthy of humane treatment. Accounts of early warfare in Europe, Asia, Africa, and other places reveal that killing off many of the defeated citizens was totally acceptable, if not actually expected, along with the looting of everything in sight. Humane treatment of the enemy was not even a consideration.

Often it is easier to demonize and depersonalize someone if they look different from us. How the white authorities dealt with the blacks in South Africa, how Americans dealt with the Vietnamese, and how our society has dealt with the American Indians demonstrates how easy it is to mistreat those who look or are different. On the other hand, people do not have to look different to be victimized. What happened recently in Cambodia and in several countries in Africa are good examples of this. These victims looked and were basically just like their killers.

Although situations such as combat and mob violence can induce otherwise law abiding and humane people to break the law or engage in violent behavior, the normal citizen usually is not motivated to do either. However, we do have road rage violence, often by otherwise non-violent people. On the other hand, the sociopathic killer or career criminal is always potentially violent or law breaking. The sociopath is anti-social, and that basically means that he is against all of society (McConnell, 1989, p.478). In a sense, he is at war with most of society.

One could write a very large book about the many people paroled or given inadequate (too short) sentences even though they are dangerous, and who later abused, raped or murdered again—sometimes over and over again. Arthur Shawcross and Kenneth Allen McDuff are but two of hundreds of examples. Of course, when one looks into it, several reasons become apparent. Trying to deal with prison overcrowding is one reason for early release. Two others are that many legislators have absolutely no understanding whatsoever about the type of people (criminals) we are dealing with and that we still have far too many lenient judges, and ignorant parole boards, psychologists, and social workers. If we insist on turning these criminals loose, perhaps they should be disabled so that they can no longer harm anyone else. We probably do need cruel and unusual punishment for cruel and unusual people. The execution of Kenneth Allen McDuff was by far less traumatic, stressful, and painful than the deaths he inflicted on his victims (Lavergne, 1999). Some say that someone who tortures, sexually abuses, murders, and mutilates several children should be given a punishment at least equal to that which he inflicted on his victims. A painless, lethal injection in no way approximates the pain and terror suffered by his victims.

While I worked in Lake Jackson, Texas with the school system in 1982, an attractive sixth grade Hispanic girl was shot and killed by her father. Her parents were separated, and the father went to the mother's home, supposedly to kill her. When he showed up with a pistol and fired at her, the child stepped in the way trying to protect her mother, getting killed in the process. Since we moved away shortly after the event, I do not know what happened in this case. However, the investigating officer told me that five years previously he had arrested the same suspect for killing another wife. And according to the suspect's sister-in-law, who worked at the school, he also had killed two girlfriends in Florida before returning to Texas. Now something is very wrong with this situation. Why is someone who has killed three people still walking around free to menace the public? This is just another example of our failed criminal justice system. We do not do a very good job of keeping dangerous people off of the streets.

Although meanness, cruelty, and sadism may be things many people are capable of, our culture should discourage them. Some cultures do, and some do not. It is our choice.

## B. Bad Cops and Bad Prisons

A TEACHER AT the Ellis prison unit near Huntsville, Texas had a running debate with his inmate students about police brutality, to say nothing about guard and guard-supported inmate brutality in many Texas prisons at the time. The inmates maintained that many if not most policemen were both abusive and sadistic. Of course, he disagreed, thinking that they had a warped and incorrect view of reality. Then one night, on the way home from work, he had an awakening experience. Possibly, he was driving a little too fast, but he soon noticed a flashing light, a siren, and a police car right behind him. When he stopped, the deputy came over, yanked open his door, jerked him out of the car and threw him up against the door. He then put handcuffs on him, roughed him up, cursing and using abusive language the entire time. Of course, never having experienced anything like this, the teacher was both shocked and amazed. The next day, when he returned to school, he told his students about his experience. After that, he had an entirely different perspective of police brutality. While the inmates' viewpoint may have been somewhat biased, there is a lot of truth to it. The police can be abusive to anyone with little or no provocation, and often they are (Choa-Eoan, 2000). Of course, it depends on whom they think they are dealing with. For example, in the early 1970's I was driving in Knoxville, Tennessee in an old 1949 Chevy pickup truck. Suddenly, a policeman pulled up beside me and hollered, "Pull that f-----g thing off the road. Gimmy your driver's license." After looking at the address, he then said, "Oh I see you're from Union County. Do you know Jake Butcher?" (He was an influential banker who was running for Governor at the time.) I replied that I did know him, that in fact my in-law's farm was near the Butcher's. At that, he changed his entire tone and attitude toward us. He talked about hunting in Union County. He talked about restoring antique cars and trucks. At first, he thought we were some poor country people in an old truck, people to be verbally abused and harassed. When he found that the old truck was just one to restore, not our main vehicle, and we knew influential people, everything was different. There is no telling how he would have treated us if we had been black.

Another area of concern is the use of torture to obtain confessions from suspects or to keep them from talking. While there are numerous examples of inadequate police interrogations that failed to identify suspects, there is also the other side of the picture. Recently, it came out that in area two of Chicago, several suspects were tortured into making confessions in the early 1990's (CBS-ABC). Many received death sentences. It seems that they were smothered with typewriter covers. In Conroe, Texas they were also smothering both suspects and innocent motorists, only there they held their heads under water.[6] This type of police brutality should be unthinkable in a democracy. Although the heinous nature of many crimes tends to support the concept of capital punishment, the very existence of coerced confessions makes one wonder. One attorney found almost 70 inappropriately convicted people on death row. The Innocence Project believes that there may actually be thousands of innocent people serving time for crimes they did not commit.

Recently, a program on television revealed a story of a prison in Georgia where the warden sent several guards from cell to cell to beat up the inmates for no apparent reason other than intimidation. In California, the guards in some prisons were putting antagonistic inmates into the same exercise yards (NBC). There were several fights, with several inmates getting injured or killed, and some inmates were even shot by guards who had set the whole thing up in the first place.

In Hawaii, California, Georgia, and Michigan several cases of sexual abuse toward female inmates by guards were reported (ABC, CBS). The Georgia Prison System acknowledged that the problem did exist, but claims emphatically that it has been corrected. It is not clear what remedies, if any, have been taken by these other states, or if the problem has even been acknowledged.

While working for the Tennessee Department of Corrections in the early 1970's, I never saw or heard of any abuse of the inmates. Older guards and older inmates did tell about abuse that had happened in the past, but there did not seem to be any while I was there. I heard that a long time ago, when the Brushy Mountain coal mine was still in operation, there were instances when inmates were killed in the mine, left there and then reported as missing. But there is no way to prove or disprove this. The mine is sealed, and the guards were not talking.

An inmate told me of an instance that happened in D-Block, the most secure section of the prison. He said that it was already dark when he heard several men, some with boots—probably guards, and some with tennis shoes—probably inmates, come down the hall and place a large blanket over the front of his cell—the only open section. Then he heard more footsteps, a brief but intense struggle, with someone hollering, "no, no." Then there was silence, and the blanket came down. The next day the inmate in the next cell was found hanged. The investigators came, and the death was ruled a suicide.

How many policeman murder people? While the exact number may not be obtainable, it may be a lot higher than most people even imagine. This does not count the instances when a policeman kills his spouse, with a gun or by other means, in a domestic dispute. And cases like the serial killer policeman in Florida, who would stop female motorists, then rape and murder them, do not count either. While they are homicides, these types of aberrations may be difficult to prevent. Although in the Florida serial killer case, better hiring practices and psychological evaluations might have prevented that person from becoming a law enforcement officer. However, he probably would have been a serial killer anyway. He might even have faked being a policeman to lure potential victims, a deceit which is often done.

Early in 1999, a representative from Amnesty International (CBS) said on television that the United States was the worst nation in the free world for police brutality. While this may be hard to believe for most middle class and upper class white people, especially those living in sheltered small towns and suburbs, there is data to support their claim. We like to think of ourselves as both a democracy and a humane country, not like dictatorships and third world countries where the police can abuse and even kill citizens on a whim or at the government's prompting, with no accountability to anyone. On the other hand, most blacks and Hispanics who live in large cities such as New York and Los Angeles are well aware of the all pervasive police rudeness and brutality. Many people still believe the O. J. Simpson acquittal had a lot more to do with getting back at an abusive and prejudiced police and court system than the guilt or innocence of O. J. himself (Tobin, 1996).

The amount of police abuse and rudeness suffered in places like Los Angeles and New York by minority group members, and sometimes others, is very well known throughout the entire world. Much has been written about it, and there have been numerous media programs covering it (Choa-Eoan). And it is not just killers, criminals, and gang members who are subjected to improper treatment. Innocent civilians who have done nothing wrong are frequently subjected to the same thing. Justin Volpe's sodomizing Abner Louima in New York in 1999 is unusual only in that he went so far in his abuse that other cops did finally testify against him, which is definitely not the norm. Most cops usually cover for each other. The four policemen who shot unarmed Amadou Diallo in the back over 40 times, also in 1999, were acquitted (Choa-Eoan). It seems that higher up police officials and even Mayor Giuliani are in some sort of denial that the cops were even in the wrong. Just as absurd is the case in Los Angeles where several policemen shot a young black girl in the back. They praised each other and gave themselves "high-five" hand signals. And these are just a few of those situations that come to the attention of the media. What is troubling about this widespread police violence is that there does not seem to be much public awareness or protest about it. One magazine article even suggested that until the white majority demanded a change, police brutality would continue to be tolerated.

Police shows, *America's Most Wanted*, and other law enforcement programs on television seldom show the negative side of the police. For instance, two policemen in Florida who beat a man to death were acquitted in spite of eye witnesses and what seemed to be a clear cut case of murder. Later, it was found that they had worked in several police departments across the country, where they beat and severely injured numerous innocent victims. Amazingly, they were never convicted of anything. How can this be? The answer may be that in their desire to support the police, people fail to distinguish between supporting the police in the legitimate performance of their duties and supporting or excusing police brutality and wrongdoing. What they fail to realize is that bad policing does not result in good law enforcement. On the contrary, it has the opposite effect, for a variety of reasons.

Another disturbing aspect of police brutality in a democracy is not only that it exists, but that people in positions of authority and the public as a whole appear not to be very bothered by it. There have been hundreds of shooting and beating deaths over the years in Los Angeles, many under very questionable circumstances (Cohen, 2000, March 6). These usually, although not always, involve racial minorities. And according to one television program, it seems almost impossible for citizens to make a successful complaint about police brutality. The police often will not even take the complaint, and if they do, they do not take it seriously.

A young man I worked with at the Post Office in Washington, D.C., whose father was a police captain, had what I thought at the time was a unique perception of the police attitude toward the public in general. Over the years, I have come to see that in many cases he was essentially accurate. He felt that his father, and most policemen, gradually come to see the whole world in terms of "them" and "us"—them being all civilians and us being all policemen. The idea of there being a generally law abiding public, a criminal public, and also the police was not clearly defined in their minds. Everyone who was not a policeman was one of "them." Law abiding, law breaking, good, bad, and other such concepts meant little or nothing to them.

Understanding that the previously mentioned attitude is firmly in place in many places, it is not hard to see how the police can regard any complaint by anyone as a threat to "us." The accuracy of the complaint, and even the wrong involved are of secondary importance. For instance, two of the officers involved in the Rodney King beating actually stated on television (NBC) that they did not believe they had done anything wrong. Yet, anyone with any intelligence at all can see from the tape that the amount of force used was both excessive and inappropriate, just as one can understand that the shooting of Amadou Diallo in New York was unjustified, excessive, and inappropriate—in fact, a totally inexcusable murder, just as reprehensible as the Klan murders of innocent blacks in the 60's and the recent Jasper dragging death murder in Texas.

When I was in the Army Military Police and later worked for the Tennessee Department of Corrections, we were taught to "only use the amount of force necessary" when apprehending or controlling a suspect or prisoner. And that does not mean using 12 men and stun guns to subdue and choke a handcuffed inmate, which was done recently in Arizona, resulting in the prisoner's unnecessary death. Of course, most of the authorities, from the sheriff to the medical examiner whitewashed this obvious murder, claiming that nothing wrong was done by the deputies. These types of incidents do not tend to endear law enforcement to the public. And knowing that the police will not likely be punished does not help much either.

Obviously, there are numerous cases of excellent police work, cases of crimes that seemed almost unsolvable that were solved. Nevertheless, we do not want bad policemen or bad police departments. One former Houston policeman advised a new visitor to the town that he was not sure who were the most dangerous to the public—the criminals or the police. That, of course, is a shame for any American city, whether it is accurate or merely a perception.

Brain mapping, which was discussed earlier in Chapter V, may very well some day be used not only to identify criminals and solve crimes, but also to prevent the hiring of undesirable people for law enforcement. Our entire criminal justice system needs to be overhauled and brought into the 21st century. One important improvement would be having efficient and humane policemen and women.

Recently, a former police chief from Portland, Oregon stated on television that 40 percent (2 in 5) policemen admitted to domestic abuse. A case in Los Angeles revealed similar statistics (NBC). Also, it seems that in Los Angeles spousal or child abuse by policemen was generally overlooked. There were very few arrests or prosecutions. Punishment, either legally or by the department, was usually very lenient or most often non-existent. It is difficult to get statistics nationally, because the police do not want the public to know. However, it is probably very similar everywhere. Forty per cent represents the admitted abusers. But how many others are there who do not admit it. This is not good. We should not have people carrying guns and enforcing the law who abuse their spouses, girlfriends, or children.

The television police shows frequently have officers from small towns in the Midwest and elsewhere telling why they got into police work. They often sound like humanitarians when they state how they enjoy helping people and serving the general public. They sound sincere, and no doubt they are. However, what about all the big city policemen who make it a habit of beating and abusing suspects, and even non-suspects? They do not seem to come on television stating how they love power, control, and abusing the public, especially minorities.

Recently, over 20 convictions in Los Angeles were found to be the result of lies, fake evidence, or intimidation (Cohen, 2000, p.30). One wonders how many other convictions in Los Angeles were bogus. Also, it came out that many of the police were committing serious crimes, even murder. It seems like Los Angeles is becoming similar to Mexico City, where in many cases the policemen are the criminals. One inmate suggested that we do away with the police altogether. Of course, that is absurd. We have to have the police. However, poor policing leads to poor law enforcement. We do not need, and should not tolerate, brutal, corrupt, or inefficient policemen or police departments.

## C. Punishment

WHAT IS THE proper punishment for crimes? Numerous books and articles have been written on the subject, so it is highly unlikely that anything said here will be entirely new. We read about children being hanged or burned to death during the Middle Ages for stealing a piece of bread. Clearly excessive! Now we have probation or one-year sentences for murder. While this seems extremely lenient to many people, what is realistic? And what does this have to do with rehabilitation?

A lot of what we do with lawbreakers is influenced by public sentiment toward the offenders and toward crime in general. But, unfortunately, much of it has to do with what lawmakers, who usually are neither psychologists nor criminologists, decide is appropriate. For instance, in the Massachusetts case of au pair Louise Woodward, Judge Hiller Zobel freed her after the jury convicted her of murder (Hewitt, 1997). How can a judge be allowed to basically nullify a jury conviction? Lawmakers made it possible. Many people, especially those in the medical profession, were shocked at her release. It is probably that such miscarriages of justice prompt lawmakers to legislate mandatory sentencing. And this is probably good in most cases. However, we also need the means of getting rid of overly lenient judges and also of overruling and/or appealing excessively light sentences.

In another case in another state almost identical to the Massachusetts au pair case, the lenient judge there also wanted to release the defendant. However, he was forced to give her 25 years to life by their mandatory sentencing laws. While it may be difficult to eliminate all excessively lenient judges, it should be attempted, and in the meantime judges need to be regulated, just as the police do. In this country there is absolutely no common sense in sentencing. Three people can commit almost identical crimes. One can be sentenced to death, another to ten years in prison, and the third given probation—all for doing essentially the same thing.

It was stated on television that in California the average time served for murder is about ten years—clearly not enough. However, that may be similar to what occurs in most states.

Tennessee has the one-year sentence for manslaughter. Texas has the probated sentence for murder, which common sense says should be eliminated. Recetly, Jimmy Watkins in Tarrant County went into his estranged wife's house and shot her. While driving away, he found there were still more bullets in his pistol. He then drove back and finished off the job by shooting her several times in the head while his sons looked on. The jury, although convicting him appropriately of murder, decided that he had just cause because his ex-spouse and others had harassed him over the phone. Therefore, they sentenced him to 10 years probation when he probably should have been either executed of given a life sentence. The community was shocked. Obviously, miscarriages of justice such as these should never happen. When they do, there should be a means of overruling them. Texas legislators need to eliminate the possibility of probation for murder. What, then, is a proper sentence? Of course, that is debatable—but probation for murder is not it. And this is more reason why both acquittals and inadequate sentences need to have an avenue of appeal, as they do in some other countries.

In fact, any time either procedures or laws get in the way of common sense, a change needs to be made, and this includes changing the Constitution, if necessary. Of course, in the Watkins case it was the jury and not the judge that was deluded by a couple of slick defense attorneys into giving this absurd sentence. Around the same time, there was another case of probation for murder in Lorena, Texas. But these are not that uncommon in Texas. One wonders if the legislators who made probation an option in murder cases had good sense.

In the mid-1970's when I went to work as a counselor for the work release program in Knoxville, Tennessee, I met an inmate with a life sentence for child molestation. He had been convicted on the testimony of a pathological liar who was also a known prostitute and drug addict. At the time I thought that this was unusual—to take the testimony of such an unreliable and defective witness and give a man a life sentence based on it. Later, I learned that convictions based on the testimony of felons and other unreliable persons are not that unusual, especially in Federal cases involving drugs or organized crime. And many drug dealers and organized criminals will testify against anyone about anything in a minute to save their own necks with a reduced sentence or other benefits.

The recent case of the California boy who raped and murdered a child in a casino in 1999, and was subsequently sentenced to four life sentences, is back in the news again (NBC). Both his parents and his teachers told how he was a model student and son, with evidently no behavioral problems whatsoever. Now that he is in prison, his parents are trying to sue the adoption agency for not telling them that the birth mother was mentally ill. (Withholding information happens quite frequently.) Also, there are some people who are trying to get him a new trial to excuse what he did because of insanity. Of course, he was not and is not insane just because his mother was. He knows exactly what he did. This is another example of why the insanity defense needs to be done away with altogether (Gest. 1997).

Before going to work for the state of North Carolina, I just assumed that murderers, especially multiple and serial killers, went to prison for life, that is, if they were not executed. Then, my first case with the Department of Vocational Rehabilitation in North Carolina involved a man who had just served four years for murdering his wife. He inherited her home, her business, plus quite a bit of money. I was surprised at the four-year sentence for murder, but I was even more surprised that one could inherit the property of someone he had killed. Somehow, I just assumed that murder meant a life sentence (which it usually does not), and that no one could inherit the property of the victim of one's murder (which is also false).

Except for a few do-gooders and defense attorneys, it appears that the general public is not in accord with excessively short sentences for serious crimes, especially murder. However, they do not know what to do about it. Just writing legislators, as some have suggested, does not seem to accomplish much, at least not very quickly. Many, if not most, people believe that our entire criminal justice system needs a complete overhaul from top to bottom (Gest). Dangerous people should be permanently removed from society. Unfortunately, this often does not happen. The false belief in rehabilitation, no doubt, contributes to this. When a killer behaves well while in prison, we often think that he is fixed, so we turn him loose. Then he kills again, and surprisingly, people wonder that happened. Probably, all murderers and child molesters should be locked up permanently without exception because they will always be dangerous. We need to admit this nationally and deal with it intelligently. John Gotti served only four years for his first murder. What if it had been a life sentence? Henry Lee Lucas, the serial killer, probably did not murder anywhere near the number of people he initially claimed to have killed when he was captured. However, he probably did kill at least ten or more. Here again, he only served a few years for killing his mother. If that had been a life sentence, several people would probably still be alive.

If we are going to turn dangerous people loose, should we disable them to render them harmless? If Kenneth Allen McDuff had been surgically blinded or had his hands amputated, he would not have been able to kill all the girls that he murdered after being paroled. Actually, he never should have been released.

We need to convict and put away the guilty. For instance, the man who shot several people in downtown Atlanta evidently had killed his former wife and mother-in-law, but they could not prove it. Then there is a California case that still has not been resolved. A boy walked a girl home from a college party, after which she was never seen again. While he probably killed her, there has been no charge and no conviction. Just south of Houston, a man suspected of being a serial killer has never been brought to justice. Several bodies of girls have turned up on or near his property (Hollingsworth, 1999).

The prohibition against self-incrimination also needs to be reconsidered. Obviously, there were several reasons why the Constitution prohibited this. However, in the interest of convicting the guilty, we need to update our thinking. For instance, the lie detector test, which is usually considered to be about 95% accurate cannot be used to convict anyone. On the other hand, eye witness testimony, which is probably only 30% reliable at best, is often used to send someone to prison.

Truth serum (Sodium Pentothal) has proven quite effective in arriving at the truth, although it is not foolproof. This along with the lie detector test should probably be used more often in arriving at guilt, especially with violent and dangerous offenders.

Someday, brain mapping might be used even more effectively. When a suspect is found, we would then get a court order, use brain mapping to find out if he did the crime and where any bodies, money, or other evidence is located. While defense attorneys will no doubt object to this, since they are often more interested in winning cases than in arriving at the truth (Gest), it will not only help to convict the guilty, but also to avoid convicting the innocent (as evidently is done all too often).

Actually, in an intelligent and humane society, all dangerous people should be sent to prison forever (life sentences), so that they can no longer be harmful. This includes murderers, serial rapists, and child molesters. Thousands of people have been victimized by inappropriately released convicted felons. If we care about innocent victims, the law abiding public, and if we have any common sense, we would change this.

It would be nice if we knew in advance who would commit crimes or act violently. If we could then remove them from society before they did anything wrong, it would be beneficial to society in general. Of course, we cannot do that. One has to do something before he or she can be punished or removed from society. It would be very dangerous to start locking people up because they might or even will do something wrong, as is often done in dictatorships. However, it would be beneficial to "rehabilitate" them in advance, if this ever becomes a possibility.

People steal because they are thieves. They do not become a thief after they steal something. There are people who will not steal anything, even if they have a need for it, plenty of opportunity, and little chance of getting caught. On the other hand, there are people who continuously steal in one way or another, even when they have absolutely no need to do so.

Murderers do not become murderers after they kill someone. They kill someone in most cases because they are already murderers. Of course, this concept contradicts some schools of thought who believe that all behavior is made primarily by choices and affected by the environment. While the environment is no doubt a factor, and all behavior does tend to be situation specific, to a large extent we do what we do because we are what we are.

There is another side of the picture. While cases of excellent police work and prosecutions abound, there are also too many incompetent and malintentioned policemen and prosecutors. I personally know of several cases where prosecutors decided not to indict or prosecute people obviously guilty of serious crimes. The other night *20/20* ran a story of a murder in California in 1998. The prosecutor let the killer off with probation, which was absurd according to the facts. However, even more ridiculous, that same prosecutor charged two friends who were with the victim with murder. Far fetched? Fortunately, a second trial found them not guilty. With a better judicial system, which we do not have, that prosecutor (and the judge) would have been reprimanded. And the guilty murderer would be retried and hopefully convicted for what he actually did.

I have talked with people, often attorneys, who think that our criminal justice system (including both the courts and the prisons) is just fine the way it is, and it does not need much change, if any. Actually, it needs a lot of change (Gest). And quite a few people agree that it does need changing. But they either believe that no change is possible, or they do not know how to bring it about. There needs to be a national organization, composed of attorneys, law enforcement people, and other citizens who see the need for improvement. When dangerous and violent people are either not punished or punished inadequately with too lenient sentences, not only is the public at risk with these people running around loose, but also respect for law and order is diminished, since bad people feel that their chances of little or no punishment whatsoever are fairly good.

Punishment is important, but the removal of dangerous people is even more important. The day may come when we can "fix" or cure violent and dangerous people. However, until that day comes they need to be permanently removed from society.[7]

At this writing, there are a lot of people serving rather long sentences for minimal instances of drug involvement. And there are both individuals and organizations who are actively working to change this. While I do not necessarily agree with this proposed leniency for drug possession or use, it does seem ridiculous that first time drug offenders are serving ten to twenty years, or even more, when murderers, rapists, and child molesters are often serving less than half that time.

The state of Michigan finally woke up to reality and passed legislation that allowed juveniles to be tried and sentenced as adults for serious crimes. Other states are doing the same. Under the previous system, murderers and other violent offenders were set free at age 21, as they still are in many other places. Most of them continued to be a threat and to commit more violent crimes. Logically, there should be no distinction between juvenile and adult offenders. One prosecutor said that if anyone could commit an adult crime, he or she should pay an adult penalty. The idea of treating juveniles differently may have some validity for non-violent offenses. However, rape and murder should always be dealt with as adult offenses.

It seems that as soon as some young person commits some terrible crime, different types of do-gooders pop up from everywhere, wanting to excuse and defend the criminal. Some are attorneys, some are judges, and some are people who have no business getting involved because they do not understand.

Two young men, one in a wheel chair, murdered a man in cold blood in Montana during the commission of a burglary. The judge sentenced them both to 100 years. Already, there is a do-gooder attorney hollering that the sentences are too harsh. She wants to appeal, saying that many others receive much less time for similar crimes (which is true), and therefore their sentence should be reduced (which is not true). Probably all murderers should receive life sentences without probation, parole, or any benefits.

# THE DEATH PENALTY

PROS AND CONS of the death penalty have been discussed for years. I recall reading articles and essays on this subject as long as 30 or more years ago. However, this year the debate seems to have become a lot more prominent. Both the opponents and the advocates have become much more vocal. To further complicate the issue, many of those awaiting execution this year (2000) have been found to be innocent, or at least their guilt has come into question (Alter, 2000). The problem has been especially bad in California and Illinois. In fact, the governor of Illinois, who has long been in favor of the death penalty, has put a moratorium on executions, fearing that many of those presently on death row may in fact be innocent (Alter).

The debate is similar in some respects to the pro-life/pro-choice issue, especially in the fact that there will not likely be any agreement or compromise any time soon. The two viewpoints are diametrically opposed, being based on unresolvably different premises.

People often voice their opinions, using them as facts to support their viewpoint rather than acknowledging that those opinions are just that—opinions. For example, the statement that "no government has the right to take anyone's life regardless of what they have done," is often cited as a fact that should be followed. However, it is not a fact. It is only one of several opinions, one to be considered, but still—an opinion and not a fact.

On the other hand, there are those (often relatives or friends of victims) who believe that executions are definitely both justified and desirable (Alter, p.35) but that they are far too easy on the offenders. For instance, the lethal injections used in Texas are similar to being put to sleep for an operation, the main difference being that the person does not wake up. As an example, the relatively painless death of Kenneth Allen McDuff when compared to the abuse, terror, and suffering of his victims was seen by some as far too easy. And, evidently this opinion is not all that rare, especially among victims and relatives of victims who have suffered at the hands of criminals.

On one hand people believe there should be no death penalty for anything. On the other hand, people think that the death penalty is often too easy, that those who inflict physical suffering should receive painful punishment as well—at least equal to the crime. Maybe the Eighth Amendment should be reinterpreted or modified to allow cruel and unusual punishment for "cruel and unusual behaviors." Or, perhaps the cruelty and unusualness of the punishment should only be limited by the amount of cruelty and the unusual nature of the crimes in question.

If all policemen, prosecutors, judges, and juries were both competent and well intentioned, the problem would be a lot simpler. Unfortunately, this is not always the case (Menninger, 1966). Often people either do not know what they are doing, or worse—they do know but intentionally do the wrong thing. In Los Angeles and Chicago, recent news reports have said that many convictions were based upon lies, false evidence, or coerced confessions. Some 60 people were freed in Illinois because of faulty convictions. If many death penalty convictions (or any convictions) are in fact false or inappropriate, then it is no wonder that many question them.

Many question the arbitrary and unfair way death penalties are meted out. They say that minorities and the poor are much more likely to receive the ultimate punishment (Alter). Wealthy and influential people and females seldom receive it. While these observations may be true and related to the concerns about the death penalty itself, the fairness in applying it and whether it is desirable or not are two different issues. One inmate who had his death sentence commuted to life said on TV that he himself believed in the death penalty, but it seemed ridiculous as well as unfair that out of several thousand people convicted of homicides, only one or two are given the death penalty. (That figure may or may not be that accurate.) However, most killers do not get the death penalty. In fact, they usually do not even get life sentences. Perhaps they should.

There is no doubt that if the death penalty is in fact going to be used, the rather random manner it is given out needs to be seriously examined. How can one man be sentenced to death, another to five years, and a third be given probation—all for doing essentially the same thing? It happens, and it happens all too often. Here in Texas, where the death penalty is given out more frequently than anywhere else, probation for homicide is also seen frequently. A high school student in Amarillo deliberately killed a young man with this car, and he was given probation (Colloff, 1999). A woman in Lorena shot and killed her husband while he slept in bed, and she too was given probation. In Dallas-Ft.Worth a man shot and killed his estranged wife in front of their son. The jury convicted him of murder, but he, too, got probation. Evidently they felt that some alleged insults by her or her friends justified probation. Why Texas, or anywhere else, even allows probation for murder is a mystery to intelligent people everywhere. But again, Judge Zobel of Massachusetts in 1997 released child killer Louise Woodward, reversing or ignoring the jury's conviction. How can this be allowed? And why was he not fired?

Obviously, one cannot prove that the death penalty is right or wrong—not to the satisfaction of everyone. Some believe that many crimes are so terrible that the perpetrators deserve to be put to death. Others feel that in a humane society, the death penalty has no place. It is unlikely that these two viewpoints can find any compromise. Many of those favoring it say that the death penalty is a deterrent to crimes. Those opposing it often say that it is not a deterrent. Since most killers do not get the death penalty, and most criminals know that, the infrequent and random use of it is not likely to have much deterrent value. If it were more certain and more quickly administered, there might be a deterrent effect on rational thinking but mal-intentioned people. Those having little or no concern for their own life, those believing they will not be caught, and psychotics and obsessive compulsives probably will not be deterred.

The solution probably is to have life sentences without the possibility of parole. Not having it may be partly responsible for all the death sentences in Texas. Juries know that if dangerous people are not executed, they will probably get out to offend again.

Both those for and those against the death penalty often agree that short sentences and parole are not good ideas for cruel and dangerous people. There probably needs to be more life sentences that mean a lifetime of incarceration. When a death sentence is commuted to life, it should automatically be life without parole. Also, there needs to be a means of dealing with overly lenient judges. And the absurd concept of probation for murder (as seen in Texas and Massachusetts) should be stopped.

# NOTES

[1]Often NBC, ABC, CBS, and other sources all deal with the same news items. When only one source is given it is because it was the one used.

[2]Both Caplain and Menninger seem to agree that there is little or no rehabilitation going on. However, they (and many others) seem to imply that there could be rehabilitation if we used better methods.

[3]It is difficult to obtain official data on Japanese prisons. Personal accounts seem to confirm the austere nature (NBC-CBS) of them.

[4]Jeffrey Dahmer, Ted Bundy, David Berkowitz, Russell Weston, Kip Kinkle, and the Columbine killers all killed cats and other animals before escalating to killing humans. *U.S. Newswatch* stated that they already had problems at that time and needed psychological intervention. This author agrees that they already had problems. However, it is felt that it was too late for intervention. It would not have done any good.

[5]Ainsorth assumes that Ted Bundy was honest with him. This author disagrees. It seems obvious that Mr. Bundy lied, manipulated, and continued to be a con man. The interviews were interesting, but there is probably little value in them as far as understanding human behavior is concerned.

[6]The famous Bradley case, shown on television, the newspapers, and *Texas Monthly*.

[7]According to a singer on the Sally Jesse Rafael show on August 10, 2000, "we have had prisons for over two hundred years, and it is obvious that they do not work. So why do we still have prisons?" This author would say that they are not going to work, if by work we mean that they will rehabilitate prisoners. They can punish bad behavior, but even more important, they can keep harmful people from victimizing the law-abiding public.

[8]Rhodes gives several examples of violent crimes from medieval to recent times. He also gives examples of violent behavior in primitive cultures. His contention is that people are socialized to consider violence as a valid option in resolving conflict. He says that some societies have much less violence and crime than others. However, this does not contradict the idea of how sociopaths develop.

# REFERENCES

## Books

Corey, G. & Corey, M.S., & Gallanan. P. (1993). *Issues and ethics in the helping professions*. Brooklyn: Cole Publishing.

Caplain, L. (1984). *The insanity defense and the trial of John Hinkley, Jr.* Boston: D. R. Godine.

Douglas, J. & Olshaker, M. (1995). *Mind hunter*. New York: Simon & Schuster.

Elliott, P. (1996).*Vietnam-Conflict & Controversy*. New York: Sterling Publishing.

George, R. L., & Christiani, T. S. (1995). *Counseling: theory and practice*. Boston: Allyn & Bacon.

Irwin, J. (1970). *The felon*. New Jersey: Prentice-Hall

Lavergne, G. M. (1999). *Bad boy from Rosebud*. Denton, Texas: University of North Texas Press.

McConnell, J. V. (1989). *Understanding human behavior* (6th Ed.). New York: Holt, Rinehart and Wilson.

Menninger, K. (1976). *The crime of punishment*. (14th printing). New York: The Viking Press.

Michard, S. D., & Aynesworth, H. (1983). *The only living witness*. New York: Linden Press.

Rhodes, R. (1999). *Why they kill*. New York: Alfred A. Knopf.

Rubin, Z., & McNeil, E. B. (1985). *Psychology/ Being human*. New York: Harper & Row.

Smith, C. (1999). *Murder at Yosemite*. New York: St. Martin's Press.

Tobin, J. (1996). *The run of his life*. New York: Random House.

Wade, C., & Tavris, C. (1990). *Psychology*. Philadelphia: Harper & Row. pp. 590-592.

Wilson, C. & Wilson, D. (1995). *The killers among us*. New York: Werner Books.

# Periodicals

Alter, J. (2000, June 12). The death penalty on trial. *Newsweek*. pp. 25-35.

Cartwright, G. (1992). Free to kill. *Texas Monthly*. pp. 90-95.

Chua-Coan, H. (2000, March 6). Black and blue. *Time*. pp. 24-28.

Cohen, A. (2000, March 6). Gangsta Cops. *Time*. pp. 30-34.

Colloff. (1999, November). The outsiders. *Texas Monthly*. pp 116-122+.

Gest, T., Friedman, D. & Ito, T. M. (1997). The real problems in American justice (from U.S. News, October 9, 1995). In J.L. Victor (Ed). *Criminal Justice* (pp. 223-225). Guilford, Connecticut: McGraw-Hill.

Hogan, T.F., Mize, G.E., & Clark, K. (2000). How to improve the jury system. (from the World & I., 1998). In J.L. Victor (Ed.). *Criminal Justice* (pp. 104-107). Guilford, Connecticut: Mcraw-Hill.

Hollingsworth, S. (1999, October). Is Robert Abel getting away with murder? *Texas Monthly*. pp.124-129.

Jewel, D., & Sandler, B. (November 6, 1997). Mischief or murder? *People*. pp. 154-164.

Kaplan, D. A. (1997). *Anger and ambivalence* (from Newsweek, August 7, 1995). In J. L. Victor (Ed.). *Criminal Justice*. (pp.223-225). Guilford, Connecticut. McGraw-Hill.

Singh, L. (2000, January). Christian media star David Berkowitz. *USA Confidential*. New York: General Media Communications.

Young, M. A. (2000). Should we amend the Constitution to protect victims' rights? (from Insight, August 31, 1998). In J. L. Victor (Ed.). *Criminal Justice*. pp. 54-57)). Guilford, Connecticut: McGraw-Hill.

## Miscellaneous

Koppel, T. (2000, April). Crime and punishment. *Nightline*. New York: ABC News.

ICBM (International Consortium for Brain Mapping). (Mazziota et al., 1995, 1995a). *Human Brain Project*. (PA-96-002). Huerta & Koslow—1997 Internet.

Sam, Son of. (1997). ABC News. *WABC*. (Personal Interview—Internet).

Stossel, J. (2000, July 14). Dr. Michael Swango. 20/20 *Associated Press*. New York: ABC News—Internet.

The Cruelty Connection. (1998, June 26) House Resolution #338. *WABC Eyewitness News*. (Internet)

# BIBLIOGRAPHY

Bender, D. L. & Leone, B. (Eds.) (1989). *Crime and criminals*. San Diego. Greenhaven Press.

Bender, D. L. & Leone, B. (Eds.) (1985). *America's prisons*. St. Paul: Greenhaven Press.

Douglas, J. & Olshaker, M. (1995). *Mind hunter—inside the FBI's elite serial crime unit*. New York: Simon & Schuster.

Furio, J. (1998). *Serial killer letters, a penetrating look inside the minds of killers*. Philadelphia: The Charles Press Publishers.

Grant, R. & Katz, J. (1998). *The great trials of the twenties*. New York: Sarpedon.

Irwin, J. (1970). *The felon*. Englewood Cliffs: Prentice Hall.

Nussbaum, A. (1974). *A second chance:amnesty for the first offender*. New York: Hawthorn Books.

Pepinsky, H. E. & Jesilow, P. (1984). *Myths that cause crimes*. Washington, DC: Seven Locks Press.

Peterson, R. W. & Pitches, P. J. (Chairs) (1973). *A national strategy to reduce crime*. U.S.Government Printing Office.

Platt, A. M. (1969). *Why they kill*. New York: Alfred A. Knopf.

Smith, A.B. & Berlin, L. (1974). *Treating the ciminal offender*. Dobbs Ferry, New York: Oceana Publications.

www.ingramcontent.com/pod-product-compliance
Lightning Source LLC
Chambersburg PA
CBHW072341290526
45794CB00002B/962